# CAREERS IN LAW ENFORCEMENT AND SECURITY

# CAREERS IN LAW ENFORCEMENT AND SECURITY

By
Paul Cohen
and
Shari Cohen

THE ROSEN PUBLISHING GROUP, INC.
New York

Published in 1990 by The Rosen Publishing Group, Inc.
29 East 21st Street, New York, NY 10010

*First Edition*

Library of Congress Cataloging-in-Publication Data

Cohen, Paul, 1948
    Careers in law enforcement and security / by Paul Cohen and
Shari Cohen. — 1st ed.
        p.    cm.
    Summary: Discusses career possibilities as private investiga-
tors, police, and in the field of law enforcement.
    Includes bibliographical refernces (p.    ).
    ISBN 0-8239-1026-1 :
    1. Police—Vocational guidance—United States—Juvenile
literature.     2. Law enforcement—Vocational guidance—
United States—Juvenile literature.     [1. Private
investigators—Vocational guidance.     2. Police—Vocational
guidance.     3. Law enforcement—Vocational guidance.
4. Vocational guidance.]     I. Cohen, Shari.     II. Title.
HV7922.C64    1990                                          90-8063
363.2'023';73—dc20                                              CIP
                                                                 AC

*Manufactured in the United States of America*

# About the Authors

Paul Cohen is a native of Milwaukee, Wisconsin. After graduating from the University of Wisconsin, he and his wife, Shari, moved to Los Angeles, where he attended law school. After earning a J.D. degree in law, he opened his own investigation business, Cohen & Associates, in 1976.

Paul works closely with attorneys and insurance companies, bringing in witnesses and gathering facts and information for various cases. Cohen & Associates is often called upon to assist in newsworthy court trials throughout the nation.

Shari Cohen also has an investigation license through the state of California. She assists Paul in the daily operations of Cohen & Associates. Shari is the author of six books and is currently involved in writing and developing stories for television.

The Cohens live in Woodland Hills, California, with their three children, Barry, Adam, and Stephanie.

# Contents

# Introduction

What is the life of a private detective really like? Do you visualize private detectives as the 1950s image of rough, middle-aged men with raincoats and slanted hats; men who chain-smoked cigarettes, talked in gravelly voices, and always got the bad guy in the end? Perhaps you think of them as the 1970s or 1980s version, the Rockfords and the Magnums; tall, good-looking guys who carried guns and lived in remote houses close to the beach.

Think again. The private detectives of today are hard-working, law-abiding citizens, men and women from all walks of life. They put in long hours and sometimes after years of investigating find their cases still unsolved.

In this book we will look into the lives and careers of today's detectives and investigators. We will also learn about other career opportunities in the law-enforcement field, such as police, FBI, CIA, Secret Service, drug enforcement agencies, parole and probation officers, and security guards.

Did you know that FBI agents investigate violations of federal law, such as robbery, organized crime, kidnapping, and terrorism? Frequently, agents must testify in court about cases that they investigate. Perhaps that sounds like an interesting and challenging career, something you might want to learn more about.

In these chapters you will read personal interviews with various people serving in law enforcement and other related occupations. You will hear first-hand what it is like to be a

Secret Service agent and be called upon to protect high-profile people such as Presidents and foreign dignitaries visiting the United States.

Finding the right job in law enforcement and security takes time and patience. It requires on your part honesty, a sense of responsibility, and a desire to serve the public. Reading these chapters, you will learn how to recognize your strengths and weaknesses in certain areas and, most important, how to package yourself for success.

*Chapter* I

# How the System Works

Wherever people live there are laws. The laws are rules that tell us what we can do and what we cannot do. We need laws to live safely in our communities. We need to be told how fast we may drive our cars or where and when we can park our cars. The enforcers of our laws are the police. The police officers protect us by making sure that others abide by the laws. Imagine how it would be if there were no laws or police. The cities would be full of crime. We would all have to fend for ourselves against the criminals. With no arrests being made and no one having to spend time in jail, the thieves and murderers would roam the streets freely. Thankfully, that is not the case.

Police officers, trained to protect life and property, are on call around the clock for any emergency. They meet every incident with clear thinking and prompt action. Many different careers are available within the police department. Before we look into those career choices, we should briefly examine how our judicial system works.

In the United States, our police agencies operate under city, county, state, and federal governments. Each agency is responsible to its own division of government. Within these divisions are jobs as detective, traffic, working with juveniles, and communications, to name a few. Within these jobs, duties are broken down even more into more specialized work. The Traffic Division includes motorcycle police work and helicopter patrol. Detective work leads into working with the criminal laboratory, tracing fingerprints and collecting evidence to be used in trials. Following is a breakdown of the various areas of law enforcement and a brief description of the duties and responsibilities connected with each.

*City Police*

City police have the power to enforce the law only within their own city. They do not have police powers in other communities. The Police Department's goals are to prevent crime, investigate crime, and apprehend offenders. The police also work to control traffic, maintain order, and deal with emergencies and disasters. Additional activities of a city police officer are to:

- control crowds at public gatherings;
- patrol areas and make observations;
- answer emergency calls;
- conduct investigations;
- write reports;
- testify in court.

City police may cover their beats alone or with other police officers. They may ride in a squad car or walk. They are on the lookout for stolen automobiles and may note any suspicious characters or circumstances in their area. Officers are also called upon to settle quarrels or to find missing persons. Each day is different; however, the work can be challenging and rewarding, and it can be dangerous. City police work offers many opportunities to help people and to serve the community.

*County Police*

The powers of a county police force extend throughout the county, except in towns and cities that have their own force. A sheriff is elected by the people and is the chief law-enforcement officer in most counties. In some states the Sheriff's Department provides services on a contract basis to cities and towns within the county. The sheriff's duties vary from one county to the next. The department may be responsible for all traffic procedures or have the responsibility for prisoners in the county jails. It may even be involved in settling business disputes and other civil matters. The Sheriff's Department is also called upon to conduct certain police operations and to provide training and local services to city police.

*State Police*

State police officers, sometimes called State Troopers, patrol highways throughout the United States. Their job is to enforce traffic laws, to issue traffic tickets to motorists who violate those laws, to provide information to travelers, to handle traffic control, and to summon emergency equipment at the scene of an accident or emergency. They also sometimes check the weight of commercial vehicles and conduct driver's tests.

State police officers help city and county police forces to catch lawbreakers and to control civil disturbances. They are employed by every state except Hawaii. California has the largest force, North Dakota the smallest.

*Federal Law Enforcement Agencies*

The main law-enforcement agencies of the federal government are the Department of Justice, the Department of the Treasury, and the U.S. Postal Service. The federal law-enforcement agencies impose taxes and enforce constitutional and federal law.

Department of Justice agencies include the Federal Bureau of Investigation (FBI); the Drug Enforcement Administration (DEA); the Immigration and Naturalization Service (INS); and the U.S. Marshals Service. Agencies in the Treasury include the Bureau of Alcohol, Tobacco and Firearms; the Secret Service; and the U.S. Customs Service. The Postal Inspection Service deals with such crimes as mail fraud and misuse of the mails.

The chart below lists the duties and responsibilities of each department:

## FEDERAL BUREAU OF INVESTIGATION (FBI)

- Deals with bank robberies and kidnappings.
- Investigates violations of federal laws.
- Provides training, identification, and laboratory services to local police.

## DRUG ENFORCEMENT ADMINISTRATION (DEA)

- Investigates cases involving illicit narcotics and drugs.

## IMMIGRATION AND NATURALIZATION SERVICE

- Enforces alien-entry laws.

## BUREAU OF ALCOHOL, TOBACCO AND FIREARMS

- Investigates tax violations related to alcohol and tobacco.
- Enforces the laws concerning control of firearms.
- Investigates bombings.

## SECRET SERVICE

- Protects the President and Vice-President and their families.
- Investigates counterfeiting.

## THE U.S. CUSTOMS SERVICE

- Investigates smuggling activities.

### Private Police Agencies

Private police agencies are licensed by the state to perform limited types of police work. Industrial security police guard factories and warehouses. Campus police are hired to protect the people and property of colleges and universities. Private investigative agencies provide detective services to individuals and businesses.

*Police Operations*

Many of you may already be familiar with the daily and nightly activities of your own police force. They are involved in many areas of law enforcement, such as patrol operations, traffic, working with juveniles, criminal investigations, and records and communications work. As we begin to discuss the various areas of police work, it is important that you know the successive steps in the career ladder. In order of rank the department comprises the Police Chief, Commander, Captain, Lieutenant, Sergeant, Police Officer.

The *Lieutenant* is typically a watch commander in large geographic areas or the Officer-in-Charge of an organizational section. The Lieutenant's position is supervisory in nature, similar to the Sergeant's but with higher and broader administrative responsibilities. The Lieutenant should be qualified to supervise practically any part of the department, including the Detectives.

The *Sergeant's* position is that of a field supervisor. There are also administrative and special assignments, but the basic position has the Sergeant working as a field supervisor.

*Detectives* do specialized or generalized follow-up investigation work. Most Detectives are assigned to the Criminal Investigation Division after several years on patrol duty. In large departments, Detectives are organized into specialized units, such as homicide, robbery, and narcotics. The Detective's job in local departments usually starts where the activities of the Police Officer end. Detectives prepare cases and evidence for presentation in court.

The *Captain* is regarded as the entry administrative level. The typical Captain position is as commanding officer of a specific area or division.

The *Commissioner*, *Chief of Police*, or *Superintendent* is the executive head of the department. This position is usually appointed by a mayor, city administrator, or legislative body. In larger agencies, executive officers may be selected through a Civil Service merit system, after moving up through the ranks from Patrol Officer.

## CAREER LADDER

Chief

_____

Deputy Chief

_____

Commander

_____

Captain

_____

Lieutenant

_____

Detective

_____

Sergeant

_____

Police Officer

_____

# Careers in Police Work

*Patrol Officer*

The Patrol Division, consisting of uniformed patrol officers, provides basic police services. The patrolman's job is crime prevention, but that branches out to all areas of crime. Most patrol is carried out by officers in police cars that are assigned to specific beats or areas of the community.

Although much of the officer's work involves disposing of minor complaints, such as family disputes and arguing neighbors, in many instances these minor calls can erupt into major ones. A simple case of domestic bickering can evolve into violence and physical abuse. A report of a crying child can lead to the discovery of serious child abuse. Every call is important and must be investigated thoroughly. Therefore, the officer who answers these calls must be professionally trained to handle various types of situations and must be always alert.

When the officer responds to a 911 emergency call, every minute of delay could be a matter of life or death. Quick response is a key to service for the officer's community; he or she must use speed and caution when answering a 911 call. Just a few seconds of delay could mean the difference in whether a criminal suspect is captured and stopped from committing further crimes.

In some cities police use "hotshot cars" that respond to only the most serious of the priority-one calls. The hotshot car system allows police to respond to life-threatening situations even before other emergency calls. In these situations, the patrol officer is the one who, arriving on the scene, is asked to save someone from drowning or to stop someone from bleeding to death. An officer who responds to a 911 call may have to do many things at once and be called upon to use his or her mental and physical strengths to their greatest capacities. Fred J. Cook, in his book *City Cop*,* wrote, "One thing a rookie quickly finds out is that the policeman is a jack-of-all-trades. If there is a family dispute, we are almost certain to be called. We try to keep the husband and wife from killing each other. We act like lawyers in the case, questioning first one, then the other, to find out what has caused the trouble. Then we try to act as marriage counselors, to get the couple calmed down and on friendly terms—for the time being, at least."

*Double Duty*

Take the case of Brian and Paul, two police officers working the night shift in Minneapolis, Minnesota. After coming on duty at midnight, they arrested a drunk driver, broke up a major street gang fight, then stopped for donuts and coffee. As they were sitting at a table, a call came in regarding smoke coming from a home just a few blocks away.

Brian and Paul arrived on the scene just minutes later and realized that they had their hands full. The lower floor of a two-story home was in flames. People were panicking, there were injuries to be attended to, and—to make matters worse—two men were fleeing the scene into the back alley. Paul set off to capture the men, who were suspected of arson. Brian attended to the injured and summoned the fire department and the paramedics.

Smoke was now billowing from the house, stinging the lungs of the police officer and the members of the family, who had rushed outside to safety. The family dog was still inside, and

---

* Fred J. Cook. *City Cop*. New York: Doubleday, 1979.

Brian saw an opportunity to go in and retrieve him. Struggling to hold his breath, he ran inside and searched for the German shepherd. The heat in the living room was intense, and Brian doubted that the dog was still alive. Suddenly he heard a whimper coming from the back bedroom area. He made his way through the darkness and found the dog curled up next to a bed, struggling for air. Brian grabbed the dog by the collar and, because of the weight, dragged him to the front door and out to safety.

Meanwhile, Paul was chasing the two suspects down the alley and over neighboring fences. He finally cornered them and they gave up, holding their hands in the air. Paul escorted them back to the house. By that time the fire department and paramedics were on the scene, and back-up cars had arrived to assist the officers.

The situation was under control, and Brian and Paul were finally able to leave the site. Like all other officers, these two were called upon to perform several emergency duties at the same time until other departments arrived.

## The Scene of a Crime

The patrol officers who are the first to arrive at any crime scene have a major responsibility—that of preserving any evidence. The detective instinct must come to the surface, and the officer's mind will be full of questions. How did this come about? Who are the people involved? What pieces of evidence are left here at the scene? How can this area be protected from the public until others in the department arrive?

An officer is in action from the moment he or she arrives at the scene. Just a strand of hair or stain of blood found at the scene can be collected and sent to the lab for inspection. The smallest piece of evidence can make a world of difference if the case comes to trial. And the smallest piece of evidence may be enough to convict a person of a crime. So it is the officer's job to notice every minute detail and act as an investigator in collecting the facts and evidence. A report is written on the spot and includes the officer's personal notations and comments.

At a later date the evidence collected by the patrol officer will be used by the police detectives and the FBI. The officer may have to testify in court about the evidence and about the scene as he or she found it upon arrival. Patrol officers must use skill and the best of their ability when recognizing and safeguarding evidence for a possible future trial.

*Frustrations and Triumphs*

Patrol officers often go on foot, checking building and doors and talking to suspicious characters. These officers are the core of the police department. They become familiar with conditions throughout their area and remain alert for anything unusual. Often the patrol officers are unable to help, as when an accident victim has died, a person has drowned, or a family member has been found murdered. The officer may arrive on the scene after the tragedy has occurred. One officer remembers:

"I've had people die in my arms. It's not always easy to play the macho part, to be strong and unmoved. I know there is nothing I can do to help them, but it's a forceful feeling. Even the ones who deserve it. . .they become just another human being who is on the way out. I sometimes think that they could be family or a friend, and I hate to admit it but I've shed some tears right along with them. I try to hold the emotions in check and save them for later, but when a guy or kid is taking his last breath, you forget about the image. The image means nothing when a brother is saying his last goodbye."

Most crime calls are answered, not by superhuman policemen and women, but by experienced, hard-working individuals. Frustrations must be dealt with in having a criminal slip away or a crime go unsolved. At times there seems to be nothing but bloodshed, murder, and theft. But there are those days when lives are saved, when criminals are captured and put behind bars. There are days when a lost child is reunited with her parents, a bomb located and dismantled, a baby delivered safely at home. There are triumphs and frustrations in every day of the police officer's life. The officer's work brings him or her in contact with people from all walks of life, and those people produce a million different combinations of situations. Being a good patrol officer means endless hard work and devotion to the job.

*Traffic Officer*

Most traffic law enforcement and accident investigation is carried out by patrol officers. In large cities, however, specialists may handle serious accidents, such as hit-and-run. Motorcycle patrols may be responsible for freeway traffic. In large cities, officers may be assigned to direct traffic at busy intersections.

Traffic officers have a variety of duties. They observe drivers and make sure that speed and safety laws are obeyed. They answer emergency calls about accidents. When an officer arrives at the scene of an accident, he or she must do many things. First, the officer finds out if injuries are involved. If so, the paramedics or ambulance are summoned. It is the officer's responsibility to set out flares around the accident scene so that passersby will not interfere. If emergency first aid is needed, the traffic officer gives it until other help arrives. The officer observes the incident and writes a report on the spot. Notations are made such as the existence of skid marks or the position of the vehicle after impact. A sketch or diagram is made, showing the scene as it was when the officer arrived: the direction in which the vehicles were traveling, where the point of impact occurred. A traffic officer can arrest a driver if he or she is sure or even suspects that the driver caused the accident, either because of drunkenness or drugs or any other probable cause. When the situation is under control and the victim has been transported to the hospital, the officer goes to the hospital to talk with the injured party, if possible. Questions are asked, such as, whose fault was the accident? In what direction were the cars moving? Did the other driver signal before turning or striking? The officer completes his preliminary investigation and later files his report at headquarters.

The officer's report will be referred to at a later date, either by insurance companies or by attorneys who may be filing a lawsuit. The officer's notations are important and may make a great difference in a person's driving record and insurance status.

The job of traffic officer may be tedious one day, being spent stopping people for a broken taillight or an invalid registration. The next day it may entail a major intersection collision involving escapees on the run and multiple injuries. Traffic officers must be able to work in all kinds of weather conditions. Their work finds them outdoors in the worst ice storms of winter and the hottest of summer days. They must be knowledgeable and trained in cardiopulmonary resuscitation (CPR) and traffic codes and violations.

You may wish to become a motorcycle officer, patrolling the busy streets and freeways. To do so, you must complete a tough two-week course. Statistics show that half the trainees in a class may fail. Riding a 600-pound motorcycle, trainees must learn precision riding and must complete turns and perform figure eights. They practice braking and must learn how to stop quickly without losing control. There is also a written exam on regulations and procedures and another on motorcycle maintenance. Once you pass the course, you are a Certified Class I Motorcycle Rider.

*Traffic Reporting Center*

A dispatcher's voice comes over the car or motorcycle radio, and the officer is ready. He or she acknowledges the call and enters the time in an activity log. Emergency lights flash, the siren blares, and the highway patrol heads toward the scene of another accident. Who are the people on the other end of the communication system, the ones who take the calls from the public and dispatch them to the officers nearest to the reporting location?

It is the communications officer who radios a police car or cycle. The dispatchers are assigned to and stay in continual radio contact with the officers who patrol a particular city area. Individuals are seated at computer consoles and direct their officers to traffic problems as they occur. They supply the officers with information on a vehicle or driver and summon aid by calling a tow truck, a fire truck, an ambulance, or a clean-up crew.

Calls come in to computer panel boards at central headquarters. Each board shows a map of a portion of the city. Squad cars are show on the board as white dots. Red dots are the cars of police supervisors. The communications operators can see the location of every police car at any moment of the day or night.

If a call comes in from a person reporting a crime, the call is immediately directed to the operator whose board covers that area. The operator coordinates all moves from his or her board. Help or back-up cars can be sent in a matter of minutes.

In squad cars, communication equipment is installed around the dashboard area. Motorcycle officers have units built into their helmet and on their cycle. The volume can be turned up so that even when officers are away from their vehicle they can hear the call and return if necessary.

Each department operates on a special channel or wavelength. It is possible to purchase a police scanner and to listen to the calls as they come over the air from dispatcher to responding units.

The personnel at the Traffic Operations Center also take calls that come in through the call boxes that are installed on the sides of most freeways for travelers in trouble.

To prepare for a career in Traffic Control, you should take high school courses in English and government, or civics. Classes in U.S. history and physics are also helpful. Physical education and sports can help develop your stamina and agility, which you will need later on the job.

If you choose this career, you will be required to take a formal training program that lasts for several months. You will study laws and jurisdictions, patrol, traffic control, and accident investigation. You will also learn to use firearms and to defend yourself from attack. As a recruit, you will learn the laws of arrest, court procedures, rules of the road, and search and seizure laws.

*Working with Juveniles*

Many convicts serving time in prison started out as juvenile delinquents. They came from troubled families and received little or no help in dealing with their problems.

The police come in contact with far more delinquents than do other social agencies. Special officers handle cases that come to court. These officers must have a knowledge of social work and an understanding of child psychology. That combination of skills is most likely to be found in a person trained as a psychiatric social worker.

The typical juvenile case comes to police attention when the officer on the beat observes or suspects criminal acts done by a juvenile. The juvenile is either detained or released to the parents. Juvenile officers look over the case and try to interview school personnel, parents, and friends of the family. Officers receive special training in juvenile work.

*Drug Abuse Resistance Education (DARE)*

An important recent program that has been developed to teach young people is the DARE program. DARE is primarily aimed at children who have not yet had a drug experience. Its goal is to reduce the incidence of drug abuse by children. It is taught through classroom presentation by specially selected and trained (unarmed) uniformed police officers.

The DARE curriculum focuses on the concepts of peer pressure resistance training, self-concept improvement, personal safety, and value decisions concerning respect for the law. Having uniformed officers teach a primary prevention program has produced results even greater than expected. The program is instrumental in achieving a safe and secure school environment.

To date, officers representing 705 law-enforcement agencies from forty-three states have been trained to teach the DARE curriculum.

Since its inception in 1983, DARE has generated national attention for its unique approach to drug abuse prevention. The classes are given in the fifth, sixth, and seventh grades. They give students information and skills needed to resist peer pressure and to say "no" to alcohol and drugs. They try to improve the students' attitudes and help them develop decision-making skills.

The DARE program comprises seventeen weekly lessons at the elementary school level and nine at the junior high/middle school level. Studies made since the program began have produced two important findings:

- Those students who completed the DARE program showed a significant decrease in cocaine use, while non-DARE students showed a slight increase in use.
- DARE students experimented less frequently than non-DARE students with drugs such as LSD, amphetamines (uppers), depressants (downers), heroin, PCP, and drugs not prescribed by a doctor.

DARE lessons focus on four major areas:

1. Providing accurate information about tobacco, alcohol, and drugs;
2. Teaching students decision-making skills;
3. Showing students how to resist peer pressure;
4. Giving students ideas for alternatives to drug use.

*DARE Lessons*

The DARE curriculum is organized into seventeen classroom sessions conducted by the police officer, coupled with suggested activities taught by the regular classroom teacher. A wide range of teaching activities are used—question-and-answer, group discussion, role-play, and workbook exercises, all designed to encourage student participation and response.

The following brief summaries of each lesson capture the scope of the DARE curriculum and show the care taken in its preparation. All of these lessons were pilot tested and revised before widespread use began.

1. *Practices for Personal Safety.* The DARE officer reviews common safety practices to protect students from harm at home, on the way to and from school, and in the neighborhood.

2. *Drug Use and Misuse.* Students learn the harmful effects of drugs if they are misused as depicted in the film, *Drugs and Your Amazing Mind.*

3. *Consequences.* The focus is on the consequences of using and not using alcohol and marijuana. If students are aware of those consequences, they can make better informed decisions regarding their own behavior.

4. *Resisting Pressures to Use Drugs.* The DARE officer explains different types of pressure—ranging from friendly persuasion and teasing to threats—that friends and others can exert on students to try tobacco, alcohol, or drugs.

5. *Resistance Tehniques: Ways to Say No.* Students rehearse the many ways of refusing offers to try tobacco, alcohol, or drugs—simply saying no and repeating it as often as necessary; changing the subject; walking away or ignoring the person. They learn that they can avoid situations in which they might be subjected to such pressures and can "hang around" with non-users.

6. *Building Self-Esteem.* Poor self-esteem is one of the factors associated with drug misuse. How students feel about themselves results from positive and negative feelings and experiences. In this session students learn about their own positive qualities and how to compliment other students.

7. *Assertiveness: A Response Style.* Students have certain rights—to be themselves, to say what they think, to say no to

offers of drugs. The session teaches them to assert those rights confidently and without interfering with others' rights.

8. *Managing Stress Without Taking Drugs.* Students learn to recognize sources of stress in their lives and techniques for avoiding or relieving stress, including exercise, deep breathing, and talking to others. They learn that using drugs or alcohol to relieve stress causes new problems.

9. *Media Influences on Drug Use.* The DARE officer reviews strategies used in the media to encourage tobacco and alcohol use, including testimonials from celebrities and social pressure.

10. *Decision-Making and Risk-Taking.* Students learn the difference between bad risks and responsible risks, how to recognize the choices they have, and how to make a decision that promotes their self-interests.

11. *Alternatives to Drug Abuse.* Students learn that to have fun, to be accepted by peers, or to deal with feelings of anger or hurt, there are a number of alternatives to using drugs and alcohol.

12. *Role Modeling.* A high school student selected by the DARE officer visits the class, providing students with a positive role model. Students learn that drug users are in the minority.

13. *Forming a Support System.* Students learn that they need to develop positive relationships with many different people to form a support system.

14. *Ways to Deal with Pressures from Gangs.* Students discuss the kinds of pressures they may encounter from gang members and evaluate the consequences of the choices available to them.

15. *Project DARE Summary.* Students summarize and assess what they have learned.

16. *Taking a Stand.* Students compose and read aloud essays on how they can respond when they are pressured to use drugs and alcohol. The essay represents each student's "DARE pledge."

17. *Culmination.* In a schoolwide assembly planned in concert with school administrators, all students who have participated in Project DARE receive certificates of achievement.

Officers who volunteer for the DARE program do so on the basis of a solid commitment to preventing substance abuse among young people. They must have a clean record, a minimum of two years of street experience, maturity, and good communication and organization skills.

The officers should be from the local community where they are known to the students. However, when communities are small or do not have resources to assign a local officer, state police or sheriff's deputies can teach the program.

The selection process generally involves posting of the available position, a preliminary screening, and a formal interview by a review panel that can include both police and school personnel. During these interviews, DARE candidates frequently reveal skills and experience that qualify them for this unique challenge in working with children.

*Officer Training*

Training for DARE officers consist of a two-week eighty-hour seminar that is jointly presented by law-enforcement and education agencies. Several states now offer DARE officer training.

DARE instructors do not use scare tactics that focus on the dangers of drug use. Instead, they work with the children to raise their self-esteem, to teach them to make decisions on their own, and to help them identify positive alternatives to tobacco, alcohol, and drug use.

Many people believe that, over time, a change in public attitudes will reduce the demand for drugs. DARE tries to promote that change. DARE instructors help children develop mature decision-making skills that they can apply to a variety of situations as they grow up. There are Spanish and braille versions of the student's workbook used in the DARE program.

The officer training curriculum includes:

- Current drug use and prevention activities;
- Communication and public speaking skills;

- Classroom behavior;
- School-police relationships;
- Police-parent-community relationships;
- Stages of adolescent chemical dependency;
- Audiovisual techniques and other teaching aids;
- Program administration;
- Sources of supplementary funding.

Each trainee prepares and teaches one lesson to fellow trainees, who play the roles of fifth or sixth graders and who evaluate the officer's performance. Officers are helped to prepare the lesson and to present themselves in front of a group, and they are offered suggestions for improvement.

One full-time law-enforcement officer is assigned for every ten elementary schools. The cost is usually assumed by the law-enforcement agency. In some communities the school department pays the officer's salary or shares the cost with the law-enforcement agency.

The DARE program for juveniles is just one area in which law-enforcement officers can become involved. Many divisional detectives handle juvenile crimes that occur at any time, day or night. The officers encounter a variety of incidents, such as robbery, homicide, and sexual assault. Often, after arrests are made, officers must talk to the offender's parents and recommend courses of action to be taken such as sending their son or daughter to a juvenile justice connection project for further analysis. There the offender may be referred to a psychiatrist, a counselor, or a medical doctor.

Often the recommendation is to refer the juvenile to a Back in Control Institute. This is done when the parents have lost control of the situation. Parenting classes are available at such institutes.

The main options for a juvenile who has been arrested are:

- To be counseled and released. The arrest remains, but it is kept low-key.
- To have a court hearing. The judge may grant probation

depending on interviews with parents, family friends, teachers, etc. If probation is not granted, the matter is turned over to the district attorney's office.

First-time offenders are usually sent to juvenile hall for a period of one to three months. This is a type of reform school, with classes and strict rules and regulations. Second-time offenders are sent to juvenile camp, which can be easy or very tough. An offender can be held in juvenile camp until the age of twenty-five. The philosophy is not to punish but to get the child back on the right track.

A very young child who commits a serious crime is interviewed to determine if he or she knows right from wrong. The child receives psychological testing and evaluation. If the crime is very serious, especially if drugs are involved, the child may be sent to juvenile hall.

Officers working with juveniles have to be totally dedicated to the job. They work long, irregular hours and become involved with many families who are dealing with serious problems.

Every officer has some exposure to juvenile work in the course of his or her work, but some officers specialize in working with young people, in trying to help them get back from a life of crime. These officers need patience and an understanding of human nature. The cases can be difficult at times, but many agree that the rewards are worth it. Children have been helped and family problems worked out.

### Training for Jobs as Police Officers

Training programs vary widely in length and content, depending on the size of the force. Smaller police agencies generally lean more toward on-the-job training, whereas formal instruction at larger agencies can last from several weeks to six months.

Typical subjects include:

- Criminal law
- Motor vehicle codes
- Arrest procedures

- Methods of surveillance
- Accident investigation
- Laws of evidence
- Crowd control
- First aid
- Armed or unarmed defense techniques

Police officers have to know how to get along with people. They must be prepared to meet a variety of emergencies day and night, and much of the work deals with problems with people: domestic squabbles between husband and wife or landlord and tenant. Police must also be able to deal with cases of child abuse, to cope with a multi-car crash with injuries, or know what to do about an old person who can't take care of himself. That is why their training covers such a variety of subjects, from rules and regulations to psychology. Recruits learn how to use a gun and how to defend themselves. Proper training and preparedness have become grave concerns of law-enforcement leaders as attacks on police officers have increased in recent years. It is important for an officer to know when to shoot and how to shoot.

*Laser Training*

Training courses have made large advances in the teaching of firearms use. A newly developed laser training course shows dramatically what happens when an officer comes face to face with a potential killer.

The tools used are a laser transmitter, an electronic vest, and a shotgun converted to fire a laser beam. The laser unit and its 7-volt battery fit into the gun barrel. The beam that it shoots has a range of about 66 feet. The vest has three full-length panels on front and back. About six inches from the top of each panel is a grommet that contains a light bulb. If the laser beam hits any part of that panel the light begins to blink and a sound is heard to warn that the wearer has been hit.

The officer in training puts on the vest and takes a loaded

laser gun. He or she is told that a suspect (another laser vest hung on a rack) is somewhere in the building. When the officer finds the target, he or she draws and fires, scoring hits on the vest. If he or she is hit the lights on the vest flash on and the warning sound is heard. The situations are very realistic, and a candidate who fails the first encounter and winds up shot is often very badly shaken by the experience.

While the scene is in progress, the action is watched by a training officer who is a certified firearms instructor. The test will show whether the officer drew and fired, or whether he or she froze.

When a rookie graduates from basic training, he or she has the basic essentials for serving on regular assignments. The officer will remain under the guidance of another officer, and in some departments he or she may continue in classes on different subjects.

After an officer begins working in the field, he or she may wish to enter a more specialized area of police work, such as criminal investigation or vice. The department provides specialized training in additional areas of police work, and courses are also given at colleges and at agencies such as the Federal Bureau of Investigation.

Training for a career in law enforcement can begin as early as the moment you decide to enter the field. You can begin by taking high school courses in law, civics, history, and psychology.

*Advancement*

Promotion comes after an officer has worked for a specific length of time. Eligibility depends on time in service, performance on the job, type of education or training the officer has, and a written examination.

As positions become vacant, candidates are encouraged to fill them. Advancement to the top-ranking positions, such as department director or chief, may be made by direct appointment, but the majority of them are held by officers who have come up through the ranks.

Large city police departments offer the greatest number of advancement opportunities. Most of the larger departments maintain separate divisions, each requiring administrators, line officers, and in general more personnel at each rank level. Other opportunities for advancement may be found in related police and protective work in private companies, state and county agencies, and institutions.

## Opportunities for Women in Police Work

Female police officers have been on the American scene for quite some time. But until the early 1970s women officers usually just wrote parking tickets and handled paperwork. Many were assigned to working with female juvenile offenders.

By the mid-1970s, however, women began to be assigned to street patrol, and they now account for a significant and steadily growing number of officers across the nation. In 1977, 2.7 percent of all noncivilian police officers were female. Female recruits now comprise 25 percent of all candidates entering academy classes.

Because of legislation and litigation, women are no longer subject to different hiring practices and inferior wages, nor are they assigned only to clerical jobs or working in the juvenile division.

Patrol is the customary proving ground for rookies, and with so many female newcomers to the field, policewomen are more likely to be found on patrol and in higher-ranking jobs than ever before.

Some prejudices still remain. An order by a female officer may be challenged by a criminal, who feels that she is less qualified physically and emotionally, and it may be tougher for the officer to get her point across.

In an effort to encourage female recruits, a number of police departments offer the Crime Prevention Assistant program (CPA) to qualified officer candidates waiting to begin recruit training. Although the program is open to any minority candidate with a need for assistance, it is targeted specifically to females to help them with their academic and physical training needs.

The program offers candidates an opportunity to strengthen their areas of weakness before entering the police academy. They are paid during training. Candidates who participate have a lower dropout rate than those who have not taken the course.

The eight-week program consists of extensive physical and psychological preparatory training, various academic subject areas, practical instruction in drill and equipment care and use, and work experience. CPAs are required to meet and maintain minimum standards in physical training, academics, and general good character.

*Minorities*

Law-enforcement agencies today offer employment to all minorities. The requirement is that *all* candidates must successfully complete all steps in the selection process. Representation of women, blacks, Hispanics, and Asians has increased. In Los Angeles the hiring record is as follows, with percentages rounded to the nearest whole number:

| | |
|---|---|
| Blacks | 24% |
| Hispanics | 27% |
| Caucasians | 46% |
| Asians | 4% |
| Females | 27% |

The table represents figures from the 1981 hiring agreement approved in the federal courts through the most recent police academy recruit class in May 1988.

*Qualifications*

To become a police officer a candidate goes through a basic selection process:

- Written test
- Interview
- Medical examination
- Written psychological test battery
- Physical abilities test
- Background investigation
- Psychological evaluation

In contrast to the old process, which could take six to eight months, candidates now have a reasonable expection of entering the police academy within a few months of entering the selection process. Candidates must satisfactorily complete each step in the selection process before being scheduled for the next step. The Personnel Department is responsible to the Board of Civil Service Commissioners for administering all tests.

*Written Test.* A 45-minute multiple-choice test, it is designed to measure reading comprehension, English usage including spelling and vocabulary, reasoning, and the ability to make common sense judgments on practical problems.

*Interview.* Candidates who pass the written test are usually interviewed soon thereafter. The interview lasts about thirty minutes. The interviewer is a sworn member of the police department, usually a supervising sergeant or detective. Questions focus on the candidate's work experience, education, ability to relate well to others, reasoning and problem-solving ability, and communication skills.

*Medical Examination/Written Psychological Test.* All candidates who pass the interview with a referable score (which varies according to hiring needs) are then scheduled for the medical and written psychological test. They are administered on the same day at the same location and require about five or six hours to complete.

The medical examination is administered by a doctor employed by the Occupational Health and Safety Division of the Personnel Department. It is a thorough examination. Therefore, it is essential that candidates be in excellent health and have body fat content appropriate for their height and weight.

The written psychological test consists of three tests: (1) the

Minnesota Multiphasic Personality Inventory; (2) the 16 Personality Factor Inventory; and (3) a personal history questionnaire. The tests results are evaluated by staff psychologists.

*Background Investigation.* Candidates are then scheduled for fingerprints, photographs, and background interview on the same day. The background check is made through police records, personal and employment histories, and field reference checks. Candidates are evaluated as to respect for the law, honesty, mature judgment, respect for others, and honorable military record. All candidates submit comprehensive biographical information prior to their background investigative interview.

*Physical Abilities Test.* Candidates who successfully complete the medical examination are scheduled for the physical abilities test (PAT), designed to measure physical endurance, strength, and agility. Following is a typical test. The tests vary from state to state.

1. Endurance Run: Run as many laps as possible in 12 minutes on a ⅛ mile track.
2. Wall Scale: Run 50 yards, then scale a smooth wall six feet high.
3. Maintain Grip: Run 50 yards, then take an overhand grip on the chinning bar. Maintain the grip while hanging free for one minute.
4. Weight Drag: Run 50 feet, then drag a deadweight of 140 pounds for 50 feet.

*Psychological Interview.* Candidates are scheduled for this interview if it appears that they will be successful in their background investigation. Candidates are interviewed by a city psychologist and evaluated for judgment, emotional stability, and real interest in the job.

When a candidate has successfully completed all formal examinations, he or she is placed on an eligibility list. After being appointed and completing a probationary period, the candidate becomes a permanent employee of the police agency.

*Minimum Requirements*

Age: You must be at least 21 years of age at the time of hire, and not yet 35 years of age at the time of interview. The age maximum of 35 years for police officer applicants is specifically provided by federal law.

Education: You must be a high school graduate or have a GED equivalent. Candidates who possess a GED must meet the current minimum requirements for a High School Equivalency Certificate in most states.

Citizenship: U.S. citizenship is not required prior to employment. However, noncitizens must have applied for citizenship one year before application. Proof of citizenship application will be required during the selection process.

Vision: Must be correctable to at least 20/30 by either glasses or contact lenses with the following restrictions:
a) eyeglasses or hard contact lenses—uncorrected distance visual acuity of at least 20/70 in the poorer eye and 20/40 in the other; or b) soft contact lenses—no limit on uncorrected distance visual acuity, provided soft lenses have been worn for at least 1 year prior to the physical examination. Normal color vision is required.

Health: You must be in excellent health, with no conditions that would restrict your ability to complete academy training and perform police work.

*Salaries*

How much will you earn as a police officer? Police salaries are dependent upon individual qualifications, experience, education, type of agency, function, branch of service and where you live in the country.

The average salary at the entry-level rank on a metropolitan police force generally falls between $25,000 and $30,000 a year. Salaries in major cities range from a low of $18,500 in the South to almost $38,000 in some Western cities. Most agencies offer substantial benefit packages that include overtime, pay increases, clothing allowance, life and medical insurance programs, paid vacations, and pension plans that can take effect after as little as twenty years of service.

An officer's pay is of two types: base pay and extra pay. Base pay is the established salary as determined by rank, length of time in rank, and length of service. Extra pay is money paid in addition to usual compensation.

An officer who is injured on the job can expect that his or her agency will provide medical care and expenses and continue his or her pay during the recuperation period.

Many benefits cover the officer and his or her family as well. The following is an example of a police officer's benefit package. Figures, dates, and time vary from state to state.

| | |
|---|---|
| *Holidays:* | 13 paid holidays a year. |
| *Days Off:* | 8 days off during every 28-day deployment period. |
| *Paid Vacations:* | 15 calendar days per year during the first 10 years of service; 22 days per year after 10 years of service. |
| *Sick Leave:* | 12 days per calendar year at full pay; 5 days per year at 75 percent pay; 5 days per year at 50 percent pay. |
| *Family Illness Leave:* | 5 days per calendar year at full pay of unused sick leave for illness in the immediate family. |
| *Bereavement Leave:* | 3 days at full pay for death in the immediate family. |
| *Health Insurance:* | The city pays $301 per month maximum for approved health plans covering employees and their dependents. This contribution will be increased as health plan costs rise. |

*Dental*        The city pays $27 per month maximum for ap-
*Insurance:*    proved dental plans covering employees and
                their dependents. This contribution will be
                increased as dental plan costs rise.

*Life*          The city pays $12 per month toward the cost of
*Insurance:*    the Police Protective League-sponsored life in-
                surance plan. This contribution will rise as costs
                of the plan rise.

*Uniform*       $600 per year to cover the costs of uniform main-
*Allowance:*    tenance and replacement.

*Bonus Pay:*    Additional compensation may be provided for
                marksmanship skills, bilingual ability, longevity,
                and hazardous duty.

*Education:*    Several scholarships and professional training
                programs are available to officers who wish to
                continue their education. In addition, the city
                reimburses tuition for approved degree pro-
                grams at rates equivalent to current university
                fees.

*Pensions:*     Upon completion of academy training, all of-
                ficers become members of the police department
                pension fund. Eight percent is deducted from
                regular pay. A minimum of 10 years of service is
                required to qualify for retirement benefits;
                retired officers must be at least 50 years of age to
                receive benefits. The amount received is based
                on years of service and the officer's final average
                salary.

*Job Outlook in Police Work*

Employment of police officers is expected to increase about
as fast as the average through the year 2000, because of the
increase in the nation's population and the need for police
protection. However, employment growth may be altered by
continuing budget restraints. Although the turnover rate for
police is among the lowest of all occupations, the need to

replace workers who retire, transfer to other occupations, or stop working for other reasons will be the source of most job openings.

Realize that you must start as an entry-level officer, which usually entails routine duties. But after a period of hard work and dedication, it is likely that a specialized career in law enforcement can be within your reach.

## COLLEGES AND UNIVERSITIES OFFERING COURSES AND/OR DEGREES IN LAW ENFORCEMENT AND POLICE SCIENCE

American University, Washington, DC 20006
Antelope Valley College, Lancaster, CA 93534
Arizona State College, Flagstaff, AZ
University of Arizona, Tucson, AZ 85721
Bakersfield College, Bakersfield, CA 93305
University of British Columbia, Vancouver, Canada
Brooklyn College, Brooklyn, NY 11210
Broward Community College, Ft. Lauderdale, FL 33301
University of California, Berkeley, CA 94720
University of California, Los Angeles CA 90024
Central Missouri State University, Warrensburg, MO 64093
Cerritos College, Norwalk, CA 90650
Chaffey College, Alta Loma, CA 91701
Citrus College, Glendora, CA 91740
Contra Costa College, San Pablo, CA 94806
Diablo Valley College, Concord, CA 94520
East Los Angeles College, Monterey Park, CA 91754
El Camino Junior College, Torrance, CA 90506
Elmira College, Elmira, NY 14901
Florida State University, Tallahassee, FL 32306
Fresno Pacific College, Fresno, CA 93702
Fullerton College, Fullerton, CA 92634
Glendale Community College, Glendale CA 91208
University of Houston, Houston, TX 77004
University of Illinois, Urbana, IL 61801
Imperial Valley College, Imperial, CA 92251
Indiana University, Bloomington, IN 47401
State University of Iowa, Ames, IA 50011
Long Beach City College, Long Beach, CA 90808
Los Angeles City College, Los Angeles, CA 90029
Los Angeles Harbor College, Wilmington, CA 90744

Los Angeles Valley College, Van Nuys, CA 91401
University of Maryland, College Park, MD 20742
University of Massachusetts, Amherst, MA 01003
Michigan State University, East Lansing, MI 48823
University of Minnesota, Minneapolis, MN 55455
Modesto Junior College, Modesto, CA 95350
Monterey Peninsula College, Monterey, CA 93940
Mount San Antonio College, Walnut, CA 91789
University of Nebraska, Lincoln NE 68508
New Mexico State University, University Park NM
City College of New York, New York, NY 10031
New York University, New York, NY 10003
University of North Carolina, Chapel Hill, NC 27514
Northeastern University, Boston, MA 02115
University of Notre Dame, Notre Dame, IN 46556
Ohio State University, Columbus, OH 43210
University of Oklahoma, Norman, OK 73069
Orange Coast College, Costa Mesa, CA 92626
Riverside City College, Riverside, CA 92506
Sacramento State College, Sacramento, CA 95822
St. Lawrence University, Canton, NY 13617
St. Petersburg Junior College, St. Petersburg, FL 33733
Sam Houston State College, Huntsville, TX 77340
San Bernardino Valley College, San Bernardino, CA 92403
San Jose State College, San Jose, CA 95192
Santa Ana College, Santa Ana, CA 92706
Santa Monica College, Santa Monica, CA 90406
Santa Rosa Junior College, Santa Rosa, CA 95401
College of the Sequoias, Visalia, CA 93277
Seton Hall University, South Orange, NJ 07079
Shasta College, Redding, CA 96001
University of Southern California, Los Angeles, CA 90007
Southern Illinois University, Carbondale, IL 62901
Texas A & M University, College Station, TX 77843
Ventura College, Ventura, CA 93003

# Chapter III

# Sheriff and U.S. Marshal's Office

*Sheriff*

A career that is both challenging and exciting is that of a deputy sheriff. The Sheriff's Department has many patrol stations throughout the county that provide people with protection. Besides protecting the inner-city environment, deputy sheriffs also help with problems that occur in mountainous terrain, in dense forests, and over water.

The Sheriff's Department is also involved in the jail system. Deputy sheriffs work as court bailiffs, guarding prisoners and overseeing trials. They work with the transportation bureau, helping to maintain buses that carry prisoners to and from court. They guard against attempted escapes and keep the incoming prisoners under control.

*Preserving Public Peace*

It is the sheriff's job to keep the peace in various areas of a county or city. He or she is authorized to make arrests. The sheriff has the power to appoint deputies but cannot delegate this power of appointment. The sheriff serves summonses to initiate litigation and executes a variety of court orders. An example is the summoning of jurors and the distribution of money or property judgments.

If a witness is scheduled to testify at an upcoming trial, the sheriff may be called upon to go the witness' place of business or home and serve court papers notifying the witness of the date and time to appear.

The deputy sheriff also acts as the courtroom bailiff, bringing in prisoners to appear before the judge and handing documents and pieces of evidence from the attorneys to the judge. The deputy sheriff performs essential police functions such as the preservation of peace and the investigation of crime, along with traffic enforcement and search and rescue operations.

*Search and Rescue*

Sheriff's Departments are acquiring state-of-the art crime fighting and rescue equipment. The Law Enforcement Aerial Patrol (LEAP) is a group of airborne helicopter rescuers who are called upon when air power is the only way to respond to a disaster such as torrential rains and flooding, earthquakes, air crashes, and desert rescues.

Reaching the scene of an accident in hazardous mountain areas can present many obstacles such as fire, wind, smoke, or jagged treetops that make it difficult for a helicopter to land.

New techniques are being developed such as jumping out of aircraft on a fixed rope. The rope rescue procedure is now used regularly to get paramedics to a site.

Two 6,000-pound-test dacron lines are attached to a harness and secured to the helicopter floor. A litter is dropped to a waiting ground team. Time is of the essence in these situations, and often there is no second chance to retrieve a victim. Rescuers must act swiftly and carefully. The rescue worker clips his or her harness to the line, and then patient and rescuer are both lifted out of the area. The process is called extraction and is directed by the onboard crew chief. You may remember the crash of an airliner into the Potomac River in Washington, DC. Helicopter rescue workers performed dramatic life-saving feats, lifting survivors from the icy water to a designated spot on the shore where paramedics and ambulances were waiting.

Other rescue missions aid in car accidents that occur in the mountains and retrieve lost skiers and campers.

Crew chiefs require intensive training and must be able to handle high-stress situations in tight quarters. New recruits may start out on patrol along with an experienced observer. As they progress past 2,000 hours they receive training in desert operations and, later, mountain rescues. Most rescue fliers have at least five years in police work. Most fly an average of 1,000 hours per year.

Pilot salaries average $2,700 a month, and observers about $2,550 a month. Mission assignments depend on flight experience, and salaries vary from state to state.

Perhaps this area of law enforcement is something that would interest you. You may have questions, such as what are the general requirements for the job or what type of exams or preparation are necessary. Following are the basic duties of a deputy sheriff:

- Preservation of life
- Apprehension of criminals
- Recovery of stolen property
- Protection of property
- Preservation of public peace
- Crime prevention
- Detection and arrest of law violators

The job choices of a deputy sheriff are practically endless. The job titles vary in each state, but most fall in these areas:

- Administrative
- Custody
- Technical Services
- Court Services
- Detective

Some of the diverse assignments are:

- Special Weapons Team
- Aero Bureau

- Marine Patrol
- Mounted Enforcement (horseback)
- Search and Rescue
- Canine Unit
- Detective Units (homicide, narcotics, vice, and juvenile operations)
- Court Services (bailiff and transporting prisoners)
- Background investigation

*Requirements*

To become a deputy sheriff, applicants must meet the following requirements, which may vary from state to state:

- Be at least 20½ years old at the time of filing;
- Be a U.S. citizen;
- Have a valid driver's license;
- Be a high school graduate or have the G.E.D. equivalent;
- Be in good physical condition;
- Be of good moral character.

Applicants are also required to pass an oral and a written examination.

The written exam evaluates reading comprehension and writing skills. Only applicants who earn a qualifying score on the written test are allowed to proceed with the testing process.

Applicants must demonstrate ability to complete a job-related work sample test battery, such as running a 99-yard obstacle course and climbing solid and chain-link fence.

The oral interview takes five to ten minutes and is an exchange of information. The grade is pass or fail. You will talk about yourself and show your knowledge of the department and your understanding of the duties of the deputy sheriff. You will be asked why you chose law enforcement as a career and why you want to become a deputy sheriff.

The interviewer will be evaluating applicants on:

- Initial impression
- Interest in the position
- Appearance and attire
- Communication skills—how well you speak and understand the English language.

A thorough background investigation is performed, including a fingerprint search and polygraph (lie detector) examination.

Candidates can be disqualified for any felony conviction, job-related misdemeanor conviction, serious traffic convictions, poor credit history, poor employment history, substance abuse (alcohol, drugs), or driving under the influence of alcohol.

*Training*

As a cadet, you will be thoroughly trained in all aspects of law enforcement. The curriculum includes patrol procedures, criminal law, juvenile procedures, traffic criminal investigations, defense tactics, driver's training, and the use and care of firearms. After passing tests of academic and physical ability, cadets graduate as deputy sheriffs.

*Benefits*

Benefit packages vary from state to state but they usually include:

- Paid holidays
- Sick leave
- Promotion opportunities
- Military leave
- Health and insurance plans
- Vacations
- Retirement plan

Salaries range from $30,000 a year for a high school graduate to over $35,000 a year with a college degree.

*Related Job Opportunities*

| | |
|---|---|
| Beach patrol | Legal deputy |
| Driver training instructor | Narcotics |
| Fire safety | Polygraph examiner |
| Firearms examiner | Process server |
| Forensic and voice I.D. | Traffic enforcement |
| Helicopter pilot | Vehicle theft |
| Homicide | Vice |
| Juvenile investigator | Weapons training instructor |

*U.S. Marshal*

Another important law-enforcement agency is the Marshals Service. It is responsible to the Deputy Attorney General and is made up of executive officers of the federal courts.

Many people still think of the Old West in connection with the U.S. Marshal. Actor James Arness was Marshal Matt Dillon, hero of the long-running TV show "Gunsmoke." It is true that Marshals used to pursue villains on the frontier, but their present-day duties and responsibilities are not unlike those of the sheriff and police men and women.

Marshals now protect federal judges and provide new identities for endangered witnesses in organized crime cases. Thousands of witnesses and their families have started new lives under the Marshal's protection.

The U.S. Marshals Service was formed in 1969 as a bureau of the Department of Justice. In 1979 it was given the responsibility for pursuing federal litigation, an assignment that had belonged to the FBI. The U.S. Marshals office performs five main duties:

- Insure federal court security;
- Protect witnesses;
- Capture fugitives;
- Transport prisoners;
- Execute court orders.

A Marshal has the authority with or without a warrant to arrest violators of federal laws. The service also supports activities of the Department of Justice during civil disturbances.

To find out more about this challenging career opportunity, check with your local law enforcement agency.

# Chapter IV

# Detective Work and Criminalistics

Detectives are plain-clothes investigators who gather facts and collect evidence in criminal cases. They conduct interviews, examine records, observe the activities of suspects, and participate in raids or arrests. Most detectives are assigned to the criminal investigations division after several years on patrol duty.

In large departments, detectives are organized into specialized units such as homicide, robbery, and narcotics. Many cases that are solved by detectives are based on information supplied by patrol officers or leads supplied by victims.

Some of the detective's work is done at a desk and some out in the field. He or she works with the FBI and criminal lab in collecting evidence in a case. He gathers articles left at a crime scene and writes reports on what was found.

A detective asks questions and interviews witnesses. He or she is also called upon to testify in court on a case that he or she investigated. He or she is cross-examined by the defendant's lawyer, and a jury, not the police, decides whether the suspect is innocent or guilty.

Detectives and the crime lab work together to gather information and coordinate their knowledge and experience in trying to solve crimes.

For a closer look at how suspects are apprehended and crimes are solved, let's see what goes on the various units of a crime laboratory. The area of work is called criminalistics.

A driver was killed in an automobile crash. Was it accident, suicide, or murder? The experts who are called upon to determine the facts are called criminalists or forensic experts. The criminalist is a person who engages in the scientific investigation of crime through analysis of evidence.

Expert criminalists with modern technology and equipment can analyze or compare a substance that is too small in quantity to be analyzed or compared by conventional methods (paint from automobiles, small metal fragments). They use microscopes that can magnify hundreds of thousands of times to study items for identification and comparison.

In the case of the crash, samples from the scene would be sent to the lab for inspection. There, chips of paint from the car would be analyzed under the high-power microscope, as well as other items such as soil and glass fragments.

These technical experts include specially trained police officers and detectives. The job is an important one because it brings to light evidence that is used at trials, evidence that may help to convict or exonerate a suspect.

Experts search victims, vehicles, and scenes of crimes. They take photographs, make sketches, lift fingerprints, and make casts of footprints and tire tracks. Every mark and every piece of physical substance, no matter how small, left at the crime scene or on the person of the victim may aid in identification of the criminal. One of the principal responsibilities of the patrolman and general investigator, then, involves recognizing physical evidence, collecting it without contamination, and delivering it to a criminalist for examination.

A hair or a few strands of fiber, when compared with known specimens, may prove valuable in solving a case.

## CRIMINAL INVESTIGATION TECHNIQUES

### Interrogation

To investigate a crime, information has to be obtained. Just as a private investigator digs for facts to put a case together, so does the police detective in investigating a criminal case. The criminal investigator asks questions of people who have knowledge of the crime—a victim's neighbor or friend or family member. Suspects are interrogated. Eyewitnesses to a crime are asked to identify the perpetrator. Experiments under controlled conditions indicate that jurors convict four times as often if eyewitness testimony is offered.

*Fingerprints*

Another method of identification is fingerprinting. The lab experts use the impression made by the small ridge formations or patterns on the underside of the ends of the fingers.

You may have had your fingerprints taken for one reason or another. If you are applying for a business license or taking the bar exam, fingerprints are required. These imprints are put on file in an identification system. When an arrest is made, copies of the suspect's prints are sent to the state identification system and to the FBI in Washington, DC. If the suspect is wanted by a law enforcement agency, a notice in the file at the National Crime Information Center of the FBI alerts the interested agency of the status and location of the person.

No two persons have exactly the same arrangement of ridge patterns, and the pattern remains unchanged through life. Many police departments are now using facsimile machines to transmit fingerprints, photography, and other information from a central file. For example, a fiber found on a screen door at the scene of a burglary may be associated with a suspect's sweater, or a hair found on a suspect's truck in a hit-and-run may help prove that the truck struck the victim.

The laboratory of the FBI, the crime laboratory, and a number of cities employ criminalists. Investigations are conducted at municipal, state, and federal levels.

It is the job of the criminalist to identify evidence as to its nature and source. Fingerprints, shoe impressions, blood samples, hair follicles, and most recently DNA matching are some of the methods used to place a suspect at the scene of a crime. Great progress is being made in the matching of DNA patterns. A minute strand of hair, a flake of skin, or a drop of blood is now enough to match a person's DNA pattern with a sample of one left at the scene of a crime.

The crime labs have many names. They are called:

- Police labs
- Criminalistic labs
- Forensic science labs

Scientists in these labs require an understanding of law and criminal investigation and a familiarity with all aspects of criminal justice. They must be able to outthink and outguess the cleverest criminals.

Sometimes the scientist has nothing more to work with than a shred of clothing or a few pieces of bone in trying to determine the cause of death. They must use their knowledge and experience in trying to piece together what happened. The experts are grateful for new technologies that are helping them in their work. The spectrophotometer is an instrument that enables the criminalist to compare colors and classification of colors. He or she can identify and compare dyes, inks, paint, fibers, and other substances.

Recently, science has provided substantial aid to crime detection. High-power microscopes are used to see even the smallest piece of evidence. Computers and newly developed lab equipment assist experts in finding answers to unsolved cases. The single hair found on a murder victim can be brought to the lab and analyzed. A minute chip of paint found on the sweater of a hit-and-run victim can lead the police to the vehicle. Anything in the physical universe has the potential of becoming evidence in an investigation. Procedures used in analyzing and interpreting evidence include the examining of firearms, toxicological and serological tests, metallurgical tests, and document examinations.

*Firearms Examination*

How can a gun expert decide if a bullet came from a particular gun? He can assume it was used or believe eyewitness stories, but because of the seriousness of the crime he must be sure. The firearms expert can determine whether bullets match a gun by microscopic imperfections that are produced in gun barrels during manufacture.

Firing a gun leaves a mark or a "signature" on the bullet. When a bullet is fired, rough places inside the gun barrel leave certain marks on it. The grooves in the barrel also leave impressions on the bullet. Two bullets fired from the same gun have identical groove impressions and marks, which are matched for a positive or negative identification.

Other parts of the gun also have individual characteristics. The extractor and ejector and the breech face come in contact with the cartridge case, which may be scarred with distinctive markings. Use and wear of a firearm contribute further to the weapon's individuality.

*Serological Investigations*

Experts in the serological lab study body fluids. Often they are called upon to determine whether a bloodstain on a piece of clothing matches the blood of a victim or suspect. Serological procedures are applied to determine whether a bloodstain is human or animal in origin and its blood-group classification. A suspect in a murder with bloodstains found on his or her clothing may say that it is the blood of an animal. Certain lab tests can immediately identify the origin of the blood and its breakdown and composition.

Most people have A, B, O, or AB blood type. Another test separates Rh+ from Rh−. Each group is based on a particular chemical substance in the blood. Blood groups are inherited and never change.

Serological tests on dried bloodstains can ascertain whether the blood could have come from the suspect or the victim. These tests provide valuable evidence in prosecuting criminal cases.

## Toxicology

Another type of lab that is used in criminal investigations is the toxicology lab, where poison samples are studied. Experts put the poisons through series of steps to get rid of all the substances that would be present normally.

The specimens ordinarily examined in cases of suspected poisoning are tissue samples from vital organs, blood or urine, food, drink, and the suspected poison itself.

When a person is found dead with no apparent cause, experts can determine through urine or blood samples if a poison is present and what that poison is.

## Metallurgical Investigations

Metallurgical examinations make it possible to identify the manufacturer of a wire or a tool or other metallic material found at a crime scene. Using modern technological equipment, experts can trace the evidence to its owner.

Metallurgical examinations can be of great value in hit-and-run cases. Often some part of the vehicle is left behind, such as a piece of fender or a hubcap. Lab workers can trace these parts to the owners by finding out what make and model of car the fragments came from.

In many cases vehicles have been located by just a metal fragment found at the scene of the accident. Examiners make a great contribution to the solution of crimes. The job requires attention to detail and ability to investigate even the smallest piece of information.

## Document Examination

A blank check was stolen and written out for $1,000. The thief then forged the owner's name and cashed the check at a nearby bank. The victim knew who the forger was and told the police, who searched the suspect's apartment and found what looked like a matching signature. Before any conclusions could be made, both documents were submitted to the lab and experts began their work. They were able to identify the signature on the check as the same signature found in the suspect's home.

The lab can also identify typewriting, inks and paper, and writing left on charred paper by using various types of high-power microscopes.

Forensic experts also include voiceprint specialists, lie detector examiners, and odontologists (tooth and bite mark specialists).

## Narcotics Lab

Police officers and chemists are employed as experts in the narcotics lab. Their backgrounds include police training and college degrees in chemistry. Many who work in this field can recognize certain drugs by sight.

In examining marijuana, for example, the lab scientist may recognize it as such but perform certain lab tests to confirm the identification. The scientist weighs the drug, examines it under a microscope, and performs color tests to confirm the conclusion.

Other chemical methods are used to identify heroin. The substance is measured, filtered, mixed, and dissolved to find out exactly what drug is present and in what amount.

## Job Qualifications

Almost all the people in this field work for federal, state, or local law-enforcement and investigative agencies. Municipal and state police departments have investigative responsibilities that include the processing of evidence. Some employ civilian scientists and technicians, but many utilize specially trained police officers in police crime laboratories. The federal government employs forensic scientists in a number of agencies, including the FBI and Secret Service.

Working alongside these highly trained professionals are technicians, technologists, and lab assistants. All lab work, however, is supervised by the professional scientists, who often testify in court on their findings.

Personal traits of those employed in crime labs include curiosity, ability to work with detail, and good eyesight and color vision.

*Education*

Prospective candidates can prepare for this field by taking high school courses in math, physics, and science. College training depends on the specialty field selected.

A degree in chemistry, biology, electronics or appropriate related field should be obtained. Course work in forensic science is offered by some colleges and by law-enforcement training programs and police departments. A basic knowledge of geology and mineralogy is preferred.

*Potential and Advancement*

Modern law-enforcement practice has an ever-expanding need for the support of science and technology. The increasing sophistication of crime detection and investigative procedures will mean growth of job opportunities in this field. Growth in population and the resulting increase in crime will increase the demand for qualified scientists. More and more women are now working in these labs.

*Income*

Crime lab personnel earn between $10,000 and $17,000 a year. Some specialists earn higher salaries.

*Additional Sources of Information*

Federal Bureau of Investigation
U.S. Department of Justice
Washington, DC 20535

American Society of Criminology
1314 Kinnear Road
Columbus, OH 43212

# Chapter V

# The FBI and CIA

## FEDERAL BUREAU OF INVESTIGATION

The Federal Bureau of Investigation is surrounded by a certain aura of glamour. Many of us have read books or seen films or TV programs based on its activities. FBI men and women have an air of intrigue and secrecy. Because the work of the FBI is highly confidential, those working in the agency may not disclose information gathered in the course of their official duties to unauthorized persons, including members of their families.

### What Exactly Does the FBI Do?

The FBI is a law-enforcement agency that investigates violations of the laws of the United States. These violations include crimes such as kidnapping, bank robbery, and extortion. It also investigates espionage, sabotage, subversive activities, and other actions related to national security, organized crime, drug trafficking, terrorism, and white-collar crime. The agency looks into infringements of civil rights in violation of federal law and also handles inquiries about persons requiring security clearance at the request of other government agencies.

Basically the FBI is a fact-gathering agency. The Special Agents collect evidence in cases in which the U.S. government is or may be an interested party. Each agent carries a commission card that identifies him or her as a Special Agent of the

FBI and bears his or her name, signature, and photograph. Each agent is also issued a gold FBI badge in the shape of a shield surmounted by an eagle.

Frequently, agents are called upon to testify in court about cases that they investigate. Although they usually work alone, two or more agents are assigned to work together when performing potentially dangerous duties such as arrests and raids.

*Origin of the FBI*

The FBI was established in 1908 as the Bureau of Investigations of the Department of Justice. Following a reorganization in 1924, J. Edgar Hoover became the first director, and the bureau's present policies were defined. The bureau acquired its present name in 1935.

The FBI maintains an Identification Division, which was established in 1924, and the FBI laboratory, founded in 1932. The agency has a training program that was established in 1935 and expanded in 1972. Called the National Academy, it is located in Quantico, Virginia.

William S. Sessions was sworn in as Director on November 2, 1987, succeeding William H. Webster. Director Sessions had been a U.S. district court judge in the western district of Texas from 1974 and served as chief judge of the district from 1980.

In 1939 the FBI was made the national clearinghouse for data relating to internal security. The FBI currently has more than 21,000 employees, over 9,000 of whom are Special Agents.

Among functions specifically excluded from the jurisdiction of the FBI are investigation of counterfeiting and violations of the customs and revenue laws, which fall under the province of the Treasury Department. Violations of the postal laws, which are under the jurisdiction of the U.S. Postal Service, are also excluded.

*Fingerprinting*

The FBI currently has on file more than 178 million sets of fingerprints, the largest collection in the world. As a result the agency has been able to house criminal investigation data and identification data on missing persons. Through a service called the International Exchange of Fingerprints, the FBI can exchange identification data with the law-enforcement agencies of more than eighty foreign countries.

The prints of arrested persons, aliens, government job applicants, and military personnel form the large part of the FBI fingerprint records. In addition, many citizens voluntarily submit their fingerprints for personal identification reasons.

The responsibility for submitting complete and up-to-date information concerning the disposition of an arrest lies with the agency submitting the fingerprint card. The FBI strongly urges all police agencies submitting arrest cards to submit a fixed disposition of the case for the completion of the FBI records.

If an individual is being sought by local police for committing a crime, a stop is placed against the fugitive's fingerprints in the FBI Identification Division. The local police are immediately notified of the receipt of any additional fingerprints. The fugitive's name and identification data are also entered in the National Crime Information Center.

*Apprehension of Criminals*

The FBI laboratory employs specialists trained in many branches of scientific crime detection. They examine and analyze specimens of evidence submitted by agents and by local law-enforcement agencies. Precision instruments and chemical and other processes are utilized in the examination and analysis of bullets, fibers, bloodstains, and other substances.

On the basis of evidence supplied by the FBI, the U.S. government has secured about 14,000 convictions of offenders during recent years, and the identification facilities of the FBI were used to locate more than 33,000 fugitives from justice. The FBI uses many different means to capture criminals.

During the past years, television has been broadcasting shows dealing with law enforcement. Recently there have been such shows as "Rescue 911," "COPS," and "America's Most Wanted." On the latter, the police and FBI agents ask the public's help in finding criminals who are on the run. A reenactment of the crime is shown, along with a photograph and description of the criminal. As a result many men and women who have been running from the law have been turned in by viewers, who are often friends and neighbors of the fugitives.

### National Crime Information Center

The National Crime Information Center (NCIC) is a computerized information system established by the FBI as a service to all criminal justice agencies, local, state, and federal. The NCIC stores documented information on missing persons, stolen property, wanted persons, and criminal histories of persons arrested and fingerprinted for serious offenses. This information can be instantly retrieved over a vast communications network through the use of telecommunication equipment located in criminal justice agencies in the United States, Canada, and Puerto Rico.

### Translators

The FBI is constantly on the lookout for translators with language ability in the Romance, Germanic, Slavic, Arabic, or Oriental languages. Translators who work for the FBI are expected to act also as interpreters. A large part of the job consists of translating and interpreting written and oral foreign language material into English.

Most translators work in the Washington DC area, but it is possible to be stationed in one of the FBI's field offices located throughout the country.

Following are common questions and answers about the FBI.

*What authority do FBI agents have to make arrests?* FBI agents may make arrests without a warrant for any federal offense committed in their presence, or when they have reasonable grounds to believe that the person to be arrested has committed a felony violation of United States laws. Agents may also make arrests by warrant.

*What is the general policy of the FBI regarding arrests by agents?* Agents do not make arrests for "investigation" or "on suspicion." Before an arrest is made, if at all possible the facts of the case are presented to the United States Attorney, who decides whether or not a federal violation has occurred. If so, he may authorize agents to file a complaint, which serves as the basis of the arrest warrant.

*Can the FBI be called in to investigate a serious crime, such as murder, when the police are unable to solve the case?* No. The FBI has no authority to investigate local crimes, which are not within its jurisdiction. The FBI will, however, render all possible assistance to the police through the FBI laboratory and Identification Division.

*On what basis does the FBI select its ten most wanted fugitives?* The selection is based on several factors, including the fugitive's criminal record, the threat posed to the community, the seriousness of the crime for which the fugitive is sought, and whether nationwide publicity is likely to assist in apprehension.

*Are there openings for minority Special Agents?* Yes. Former FBI Director William H. Webster has stated, "Substantial representation of minorities and females in our ranks is right and just. Moreover, it is sound from an operations standpoint. We must represent all our citizens in order to gain the cooperation necessary in our investigations."

*What are the qualifications for FBI Special Agent?* Applicants must be citizens of the United States, willing and available to serve in any part of the United States or Puerto Rico. They must have reached their 23rd but not 35th birthday on the date of entry on duty. They must be in excellent physical condition. Applicants must possess either a law degree with a minimum of two years of resident undergraduate college work or a four-year accounting degree. The FBI considers applicants having a four-year resident college degree with fluency in a language for which the bureau has need, or three years of experience of a professional, executive, complex investigative, or other specialized nature. Applicants who have a master's or doctoral degree in physical science, or a bachelor's degree plus three years of scientific experience in a physical science may also be considered.

*What other jobs are there in the FBI?* The investigative work in the FBI is performed by Special Agents, but there are many other jobs of a support nature that are vital to the Bureau's operations. Secretary, typist, file clerk, computer programmer, fingerprint examiner, laboratory technician, radio maintenance technician, and receptionist are only a few of the positions filled by noninvestigative personnel.

*Training*

Each newly appointed Special Agent receives about sixteen weeks of training at the FBI Academy at the U.S. Marine Corps base in Quantico, Virginia, before being assigned to a field office. During this period, agents receive intensive training in defense tactics, use of firearms, and physical fitness. Agents are thoroughly schooled in federal criminal law and procedures, FBI rules and regulations, fingerprinting, and investigatory work. Agents receive regular salaries while in training.

After being assigned to a field office, the new agent usually works closely with an experienced agent for about two weeks before handling any assignments independently. The following chart is used by the Bureau for physical fitness testing.

### NEW AGENTS' PHYSICAL FITNESS TESTS AND RATING SCALE

| **MEN** | | **WOMEN** | |
|---|---|---|---|
| **Pull-Ups** | | **Modified Pull-Ups** | |
| Number Completed | Points | Number Completed | Points |
| 2–3 | 1 | 10–11 | 1 |
| 4–5 | 2 | 12–13 | 2 |
| 6–7 | 3 | 14–15 | 3 |

| **Pull-Ups** | | **Modified Pull-Ups** | |
|---|---|---|---|
| Number Completed | Points | Number Completed | Points |
| 8–9 | 4 | 16–17 | 4 |
| 10–11 | 5 | 18–19 | 5 |
| 12–13 | 6 | 20–21 | 6 |
| 14–15 | 7 | 22–23 | 7 |
| 16–17 | 8 | 24–25 | 8 |
| 18–19 | 9 | 26–27 | 9 |
| 20 or more | 10 | 28 or more | 10 |

| **Push-Ups** | | **Push-Ups** | |
|---|---|---|---|
| Number Completed | Points | Number Completed | Points |
| 25–30 | 1 | 14–17 | 1 |
| 31–35 | 2 | 18–21 | 2 |
| 36–40 | 3 | 22–25 | 3 |
| 41–45 | 4 | 26–29 | 4 |
| 46–50 | 5 | 30–33 | 5 |
| 51–55 | 6 | 34–37 | 6 |
| 56–60 | 7 | 38–41 | 7 |
| 61–65 | 8 | 42–45 | 8 |
| 66–70 | 9 | 46–49 | 9 |
| 71 or more | 10 | 50 or more | 10 |

| **Sit-Ups** | | **Sit-Ups** | |
|---|---|---|---|
| Number Completed | Points | Number Completed | Points |
| 46–51 | 1 | 46–51 | 1 |
| 52–57 | 2 | 52–57 | 2 |
| 58–63 | 3 | 58–63 | 3 |
| 64–69 | 4 | 64–69 | 4 |
| 70–75 | 5 | 70–75 | 5 |
| 76–81 | 6 | 76–81 | 6 |
| 82–87 | 7 | 82–87 | 7 |
| 88–93 | 8 | 88–93 | 8 |
| 94–99 | 9 | 94–99 | 9 |
| 100 or more | 10 | 100 or more | 10 |

| **120-Yard Shuttle Run** | | **120-Yard Shuttle Run** | |
|---|---|---|---|
| Time | Points | Time | Points |
| 25.1–26.0 | 1 | 28.1–29.0 | 1 |
| 24.6–25.0 | 2 | 27.6–28.0 | 2 |

| 120-Yard Shuttle Run | | 120-Yard Shuttle Run | |
|---|---|---|---|
| Time | Points | Time | Points |
| 24.1–24.5 | 3 | 27.1–27.5 | 3 |
| 23.6–24.0 | 4 | 26.6–27.0 | 4 |
| 23.2–23.5 | 5 | 26.1–26.5 | 5 |
| 22.8–23.1 | 6 | 25.6–26.0 | 6 |
| 22.4–22.7 | 7 | 25.1–25.5 | 7 |
| 22.0–22.3 | 8 | 24.6–25.0 | 8 |
| 21.6–21.9 | 9 | 24.1–24.5 | 9 |
| 21.5 or less | 10 | 24.0 or less | 10 |
| **Two-Mile Run** | | **Two-Mile Run** | |
| Time | Points | Time | Points |
| 15:49–16:30 | 1 | 17:56–18:45 | 1 |
| 15:24–15:48 | 2 | 17:21–17:55 | 2 |
| 14:55–15:23 | 3 | 17:01–17:20 | 3 |
| 14:26–14:54 | 4 | 16:31–17:00 | 4 |
| 13:57–14:25 | 5 | 15:51–16:30 | 5 |
| 13:28–13:56 | 6 | 15:31–15:50 | 6 |
| 12:59–13:27 | 7 | 15:01–15:30 | 7 |
| 12:30–12:58 | 8 | 14:31–15:00 | 8 |
| 12:01–12:29 | 9 | 13:46–14:30 | 9 |
| 12:00 or less | 10 | 13:45 or less | 10 |

*Salaries*

The entrance salary for FBI Special Agents is about $20,000 a year. Under specific conditions, agents may receive overtime pay up to about $5,100 a year. Special Agents are not appointed under federal Civil Service regulations; however, they receive periodic within-grade salary increases if their work performance is satisfactory. They can advance in grade as they gain experience. Salaries of supervisory agents start at over $37,000 a year. Agents receive paid vacations, sick leave, and annuities on retirement. They are required to retire at age 55 if they have served for at least 20 years. Some 58 percent of Special Agents have ten or more years of service. They frequently work longer than the customary 40-hour workweek. Employment is expected to increase with growing FBI responsibilities.

*Additional Information*

- All administrative and supervisory jobs are filled from within by selection of agents who have demonstrated the ability to assume more responsibility.
- Most agents are assigned to the 59 field offices located throughout the U.S. and in Puerto Rico. They work in cities where field office headquarters are located or in resident agencies established under field office supervision.
- Some agents are assigned to the Bureau's headquarters in Washington, DC, which supervises all FBI activities.
- FBI duties call for some travel, as agents are assigned wherever they are needed in the U.S. or in Puerto Rico.

For further information regarding this career opportunity write to:

> Federal Bureau of Investigation
> U.S. Department of Justice
> Washington, DC 20535

## CENTRAL INTELLIGENCE AGENCY

The Central Intelligence Agency (CIA) gathers facts and makes decisions based on those facts. The agency collects and evaluates information from foreign intelligence. It analyzes data from all over the world that might affect the interests of the United States. The information collected provides a basis upon which U.S. policymakers can make decisions regarding national security and events overseas.

The CIA also employs intelligence analysts, economists, and other specialists in science and technology. They assist with additional information regarding other governments. There are various career opportunities within this field, such as:

- Computer science
- Economics
- Foreign area studies
- Mathematics

- Languages
- Psychology
- Physical science
- Library science

Since its creation in 1947, the CIA has become the backbone of the world's largest intelligence community. The CIA offers the opportunity to travel throughout the world, helping to gather information about military, political, and economic conditions in other countries. CIA agents also observe agents from other countries and report their observations to the President and other high officials. Our own nation's security often depends on information that our intelligence officers supply.

The head of the CIA is the Director of Central Intelligence (DCI), who is appointed by the President with the advice and consent of the Senate. The DCI appoints other staff members and coordinates all U.S. intelligence activities.

*Inside the CIA*

The operating units of the CIA are:

- Administration
- Science and Technology
- Operations
- Intelligence

The Director of Administration runs the agency's day-to-day operations, handling personnel, finances, medical services, and employee training. An important function is the protection of the agency's facilities and guarding of information from discovery by enemy agents. This function is called counterintelligence. Counterintelligence performs security checks on employees and their families and guards the facilities with security cameras and other equipment.

The Director of Science and Technology informs the agency of the latest scientific and technological advances. The office supplies technical information to the various departments of the CIA and also develop new devices for officers to use in the field.

The Director of Operations collects intelligence. Very little is known about the activities of this department, as it is top secret.

The Director of Intelligence runs the analytical branch of the CIA. The director gathers information and writes reports on its findings and evaluation.

*Qualifications, Education, and Training*

General qualifications for working for the CIA include good character, intelligence, and resourcefulness. The agency also looks for people with a willingness to accept responsibility and a strong motivation for public service. Applicants should be willing to work overseas if necessary and must be aware that their work must often remain anonymous. Some CIA undercover agents live under assumed names and changed identities.

Although many people apply for CIA jobs, about 80 percent of applicants never get as far as an interview. The few who make it past the interview must take a lie detector test. If they pass that, they are required to take a physical exam.

United States citizenship is required. An undergraduate or graduate degree in an appropriate field is necessary, and related work experience is a plus.

Some colleges and universities take part in a cooperative education program with the CIA. Interested undergraduates who are majoring in such fields as engineering, physics, computer science, mathematics, business administration, or accounting may spend part of their time in a cooperative work/study program. The CIA also has a summer intern program available to a limited number of graduate students. Foreign language ability is useful but not essential for this program.

Applicants for clerical positions must meet the basic requirements for specific jobs and must take an aptitude test. A background security investigation is made on all accepted applicants before they are assigned to duty. Because this investigation takes time, applicants should apply well in advance of the time they wish to start working.

*Potential and Advancement*

Although the CIA employs a wide variety of people in many fields, active recruitment for specific jobs varies from year to year.

The CIA offers advancement opportunities to all employees. Formal on-the-job training is available during early and mid-career stages, and professional-level training is given within the CIA and also at other government training establishments, colleges, and universities.

For clerical employees, the CIA's Office of Training offers courses in administrative procedures, writing, employee development, and supervision and management. Off-campus courses are offered by some universities and by specialized schools at CIA headquarters. Tuition costs for approved job-related courses are paid by the CIA. Foreign language study is provided for those who are to serve overseas.

*Salaries*

Employees of the CIA are paid according to the federal government scale (GS). Starting salaries range from $20,000 to $28,000, depending on qualifications. Starting salaries for clerical workers are in the $12,000 a year range. Those working overseas receive government allowances including transportation and housing.

*Additional Sources of Information*

If you are planning to enter college or are already enrolled, see your placement officer and ask for an interview with the CIA representative who visits your campus from time to time, or whose regional office may be situated nearby. Write to:

Director of Personnel
Central Intelligence Agency
Washington, DC 20505

Enclose a résumé of your education and experience and ask for preliminary application forms.

You may call 703/351-2028 to hear a recording from the CIA regarding job openings and application procedures. Visit the CIA Recruitment Office at the Ames Center Building, 1820 North Fort Myer Drive, Arlington (Rosslyn), Virgina. No appointment is necessary; however, call for visiting hours.

*Chapter* **VI**

# Secret Service Agents

In view of the recent wave of terrorism and assassination attempts, the need for a dedicated, highly trained force to protect our government leaders has become more apparent. Secret Service agents are best known for their role in providing this protection. They are also responsible for investigating cases of counterfeiting and forgery.

This is a unique and interesting field, but it is not available to just anyone who applies. Applicants must go through months (and sometimes years) of interviews, examinations, and background checks, and then wait for a job opening.

The service's more than 1,900 special agents rotate throughout their careers between investigative and protective assignments. They are authorized to protect the following:

- The President of the United States and immediate family.
- The Vice President and immediate family or other officer in order of succession to the Presidency.
- The President-elect, Vice President-elect, and immediate families.
- Former Presidents and their spouses for life, except that protection of spouse terminates in the event of remarriage.
- Children of former Presidents until the age of sixteen.
- Major Presidential and Vice Presidential candidates and, within 120 days of the Presidential election, the spouses of such candidates.

- Visiting heads of foreign states and their spouses traveling with them.
- Distinguished foreign visitors to the U.S. and official representatives of the U.S. performing special missions abroad.

*How Protection Works*

When a person needing protection plans to visit a city or town, a lead advance agent is assigned to draw up a security plan. Let's say that Princess Caroline of Monaco is planning to make a stop in Los Angeles to attend a charity ball. Plans for her arrival would begin months earlier.

The Secret Service would want to know every detail, such as what route she would be traveling, where she would be staying, and even where her table would be located at the dinner and dance. The lead agent would begin by forming a special team that would work closely together throughout the planning stages and with other personnel of the nearest district office.

Each site that the Princess was scheduled to visit would be visited ahead of time by this special team. They would determine how many agents would be needed at any given spot, what (if any) equipment would be needed, and other requirements to assure the Princess' safety. Hospitals and evacuation routes would be gone over. Fire, ambulance, and other public service personnel would be alerted to the time of the Princess' arrival.

Agents spend many hours with famous and high-profile people. They are responsible for detering potential attackers who may lurk in a crowd. Agents are equipped with uniforms and communication systems, such as walkie-talkies, and they do carry firearms. The agents are highly visible. If many security agents are in sight, it is less likely that someone will try to harm the visitor.

*Uniformed Division*

The men and women of the Secret Service Uniformed Division are an important part of the service's protective program.

First established in 1922 as the White House Police, they were renamed in 1977.

Uniformed Division officers in the White House branch are responsible for security at the Executive Mansion and grounds and the Treasury Building and Annex. They screen visitors and patrol the White House grounds.

Their most important job is to see that the President is exposed to as little danger as possible. That involves keeping him away from angry protesters and unruly crowds. It is the agents' responsibility to screen those who will be close to the President. The job requires excellent vision and quick reflexes; so much can happen in just a few seconds that the agent must be alert at all times.

Besides protecting the President when he travels, uniformed security agents also are assigned to protect members of the President's immediate family and the White House. Many agents prefer this duty because fewer pressures are involved. In protecting the family members, the Secret Service is concerned about the possibility of kidnapping. If there are school children in the First Family, agents are assigned to accompany them to classes. Amy Carter, daughter of former President Jimmy Carter, was often photographed at her elementary school classroom with a Secret Service agent sitting nearby.

Uniformed officers carry out their White House patrol duties through foot and vehicular patrols, fixed posts, and sometimes canine teams that respond to bomb threats, suspicious packages, and other situations where explosives detection is necessary.

Overseas Presidential or Vice Presidential trips often keep Secret Service agents away from home for four to six weeks at a time. Former agent Marty Venker wrote a book about his experiences protecting the President. Venker wrote, "The hardest part is skipping across time zones. Say you're on a midnight shift to L.A., standing outside the President's door when he's sleeping. As soon as you're off, you board a plane to Boston. You try to get some sleep on the plane, but somebody's always laughing and waking you up. Three time zones later, you land in Boston near 7:00 p.m. You've got only a couple of hours before you're on duty again at midnight. After a while clocks just become decorative objects."*

The Foreign Missions branch of the Uniformed Division safeguards foreign diplomatic missions in the Washington area. Officers maintain foot and cruiser patrol in areas where embassies are located. They are assigned to fixed posts at locations where a threat has been received or at installations of countries involved in tense international situations. This branch also provides security at Blair House when foreign dignitaries are in residence.

*Treasury Police Force*

The public most often sees the Secret Service performing its mission of protecting the President or other top officials of the government. However, the majority of the almost 2,000 agents employed in the Secret Service spend most of their time protecting U.S. currency against counterfeiting. Technological advances in the printing industry have made that job more important than ever. With the printing equipment available today, an experienced printer can turn out money that would fool anyone but an expert.

Treasury security officers are also responsible for security at the main Treasury Building and the Treasury Annex and at the office of the Secretary of the Treasury. They have investigative and special arrest powers in connection with law violations in the Treasury Department, including forgery and fraudulent negotiation of government checks, bonds, and securities. Women are employed in all these categories.

These special agents must deal with everything from counterfeiting run by small-town hoodlums to big-time organized crime. They are closely involved in almost every phase of the Service's protective mission.

---

* *Confessions of an Ex-Secret Service Agent*, by Marty Venker. Donald Fine, New York, 1988.

In earlier years officers accompanied money shipments from the Bureau of Engraving and Printing, guarded currency in the Treasury Vault, and ensured the security of those doing business in the Treasury Building's cash room. These activities have changed substantially over the years. Today officers of the Treasury Police Force monitor security twenty-four hours a day at the Treasury Building. They also guard the offices of the Secretary of the Treasury and assist in the investigation of crimes.

*Qualifications, Education, and Training of Special Agents*

Special agents may be employed at Secret Service headquarters in Washington, DC, or at one of over 100 field offices throughout the United States.

If you think that you might be interested in this job opportunity, realize the following:

- Special agents must be willing to work wherever they are assigned and are subject to frequent reassignment. Because the protective responsibilities of the Secret Service go around the clock, all agents and officers perform some shift work.
- Competition is tough. Only a limited number of the best qualified applicants reach the interview stage. Applicants are rated on personal appearance, manner, ability to speak logically and effectively, and ability to adapt.
- Applicants who are selected must be prepared to wait for a vacancy to occur. During this time the applicant's background check is being completed.
- A limited number of the best-qualified applicants receive a series of in-depth interviews and must take a polygraph examination.

Appointees must be less than thirty-five years of age at the time of entrance on duty.

Applicants must have a bachelor's degree or a minimum of three years of experience, of which at least two are in criminal investigation, or a comparable combination of experience and education. College-level study in any major field is acceptable.

Applicants must pass a comprehensive medical examination prior to appointment. Weight must be in proportion to height. Vision requirements are 20/40 in each eye, correctable to 20/20.

*Promotional Opportunities*

Special agents are appointed at the GS-5 or GS-7 level, depending upon experience and education. Eligibility for promotion is based upon performance. The full performance level for a Special agent is GS-12. Selection for promotion to positions above the GS-12 level is based on merit and as vacancies occur.

*Benefits*

Low-cost health and life insurance may be obtained through federal employee programs. Immediate families may be included in health benefit plans.

Financial protection is provided, without cost, to agents and their families in the event of job-related injury or death.

Annual leave accrues at the rate of 13 to 26 days annually, based on length of employment. Prior federal civilian or military service is creditable.

Sick leave accumulates at the rate of 13 days per year without limit.

*Training*

Once active duty begins, special agents receive general investigative training at the Federal Law Enforcement Training Center in Brunswick, Georgia, and specialized training at the Secret Service facilities in Washington.

If selected to serve on the force, you will study protective techniques, criminal law, investigative procedures and devices, document and handwriting examinations, first aid, the use of firearms, and various arrest techniques. You will also receive on-the-job training. Advanced in-service training programs continue throughout an agent's career.

*Income*

Special agents are paid under the General Schedule and start at the GS-5 level, $14,390 a year, or the GS-7 level, $17,824. Agents are eligible for retirement at age 50 with 20 years of service.

The Secret Service reports that less than 3 percent of those who become agents leave before retirement, and most of those drop out within the first year or two. The average agent leaves at the mandatory retirement age, 55.

*Potential for Advancement*

From time to time the Service may actively recruit for a specific job category, but for the most part job opportunities are limited. The extremely high public interest in this work means that only the most highly qualified applicants are considered for appointment. The Secret Service has many more applicants than it has openings, but for those with a strong desire to enter this field, it is worth taking the necessary steps to apply and to be patient in waiting for an opening to occur. You can begin by taking courses in high school such as political science and civics and read additional material that is available regarding jobs in the Secret Service.

The Secret Service promotes women and minorities in all jobs. Many agents were former athletes, and some have law and graduate degrees.

Related specialty fields include electronics, engineers, communication technicians, computer experts, polygraph examiners, forensic experts, and research psychologists.

*Where to Apply*

Candidates may apply to the nearest U.S. Office of Personnel Management or Secret Service field office. The nearest area office of the U.S. Civil Service Commission can supply information on examination schedules. Or you can write to:

United States Secret Service
Personnel Division
1800 G Street, NW
Washington, DC 20223

# Chapter VII

# Parole and Probation Officers

## *PAROLE OFFICERS*

Parole is a privilege granted to prisoners in recognition of past conduct, both in prison and earlier. You may have heard about a person serving time who was paroled for "good behavior." In essence, it means that the offender was released before his or her prison term had expired. During the parole period, the parolee is required to report from time to time to prison authorities or to a parole officer to whose custody he or she was assigned when released.

Like any social worker, the parole officer is primarily interested in the rehabilitation of the offender. When a parolee engages in illegal activity, it is the parole officer's responsibility to alert the authorities and to protect society.

Violations are based upon the failure of the offender to comply with the conditions of the parole, such as not remaining in a specific place, not reporting to the officer, or committing a new crime or offense. If a violation does occur, the officer may have the parolee arrested and placed in custody pending investigation and a final decision by the parole board.

When the parole officer succeeds in rehabilitating the parolee and removing him or her from a life of crime, he or she is in effect saying society from the further cost of apprehending and detaining the offender again.

Often the parole officer is called upon to play two roles, that of friend and social worker and that of police or detective. It is not an easy job. On one hand the officer tries to help the parolee find a place in society. The officer may be the parolee's only outside contact, and a relationship of friendship and trust can develop between the two. The officer can help the ex-offender find a job or get job training. The officer arranges for welfare or other public assistance for the family if necessary and provides a helping hand in any way possible to aid the parolee. The parole officer's main concern is helping the parolee to go straight instead of returning to a life of crime.

On the other hand, however, the officer also has the duty to watch closely over the parolee and to police his or her activities in the outside world. If the officer suspects that the parolee is violating or planning to violate the conditions of parole, action must be taken. The officer needs to be sure that the parolee is not planning to flee the state or country or engage in any illegal activities.

*How Parole Works*

To illustrate the parole procedure, the successive steps follow.

- On arrival at jail the inmate is informed of the meaning of parole, how it is earned, and how he or she must behave while on parole. The inmate learns that earning parole requires good behavior and positive effort.
- Institution personnel prepare the inmate's case for the parole hearing. This involves compiling progress reports, psychological findings, medical reports, and personality evaluations.
- At the parole hearing all the information regarding the prisoner's case is studied. Parole may be approved, denied, or deferred, or no action may be taken.
- If parole is approved, plans are initiated by the board. This involved planning for a home and a job for the offender and the assigning of a parole officer.

- The prisoner is released under the supervision of the parole staff. Conditions are attached, usually that the parolee must report to the parole officer at certain times and that he/she may not leave the state, move to another residence, take another job, or get married or divorced without permission from the parole office or parole board. The parolee is required to lead a law-abiding life and to avoid places and people of questionable character.
- The parole officer make periodic visits to the parolee and checks with other family members, friends, and employer regarding the parolee's behavior and activities. The officer writes a report of the parolee's activities.
- Supervision by the parole officer is gradually eased. There are less frequent visits, reports, and fewer restrictions.
- The parolee is discharged from parole either at the expiration of the prison sentence or by action of the parole board prior to the expiration date.
- Certification of rehabilitation is issued by the parole board when the parolee has maintained a satisfactory record for a required term of years after release from confinement.

## *PROBATION OFFICER*

The probation officer supervises the offender for the probation period, which is fixed by the court and by law. During this period, the offender must not commit a criminal offense and must report to the probation office at regular intervals. In the course of his or her work, the probation officer deals with teachers, chaplains, rabbis, social workers, counselors, employers, and community organizations.

This job requires initiative and an understanding of human relationships. It is the officer's job to treat and help the offender, not to judge him or her. Because it is possible that the offender may repeat his or her acts, the probation officer must be on guard. Restrictions are therefore placed upon the offender's activities during the probation period.

*Working with Juveniles*

Perhaps one of the most important areas of work of the probation officer is with juveniles. Officers deal with juvenile delinquents and first offenders, who are often released by the court, subject to supervision, instead of being sentenced to jail or prison.

The officer tries to establish a rapport with the children and teenagers who have been in trouble with the law. He or she discusses the juvenile's problems and tries to get them back on the right track.

Probation officers do this through a process of reeducation and redirection. Besides monitoring the juvenile's activities, the officer writes a report for the court on his/her progress. The following are areas that the officer delves into when writing the report:

- *A description of circumstances*, such as what the juvenile did that got him in trouble with the law. Was the child placed in detention? What is the child's attitude toward his/her situation?
- *A record of information* about the child's parents and immediate family. What is the father like? What is the mother like? How do the siblings in the home get along?
- *Child's social and development history*. Does the child have any physical or mental handicaps? Are there any unusual circumstances in the child's development rate? How does he/she relate to friends? What type of discipline is used in the home? Is there a clash of methods used?
- *Education progress and maturity*. How is the child doing in school? Does he get along with his teachers and those in authority? Is he/she involved in sports? What type of friends does the child have?
- *Work history*. What kind of jobs has the child worked at? Did he/she get along with the employer and the other employees? Was he/she on time and responsible in the job?

The probation officer takes everything into consideration when writing a report. If the home conditions are less than adequate and there are financial problems, it will affect the child if placed back in the home while on probation. The probation officer also makes recommendations as to what steps may be taken to help the child in the future.

The reports are objective and are intended to aid the court in making an intelligent disposition of a case. The officer is not required to secure evidence as to the guilt or innocence of a person. However, if negative evidence is brought to the officer's attention, it should be reported to the authorities.

A probation officer's case load can sometimes be a hindrance to the effectiveness of his or her work. Many parole and probation officers must keep track of up to 100 assigned cases, which makes it difficult to give each person the attention and help that are necessary.

The rewards are great, however, when a parole or probation officer is able to help someone get back on the right track. By lending an understanding ear and offering assistance, the officer can be the means of changing a person's life for the better.

*Qualifications, Education, and Training*

A number of parole and probation officers come from the ranks of police officers. People who work in this field need training and experience in sociology, psychology, and criminology. Those who start out as police officers usually acquire additional training in these fields through college courses.

Requirements vary. Some states require a degree, sometimes in a specific field. Personal characteristics of understanding, objectivity, good judgment, and patience are necessary. Good communication skills and the ability to motivate people are very important. High school courses should include the social sciences, English, and history. A bachelor's degree in criminal justice, the social sciences, or a related field is required in nearly all systems.

*Potential and Advancement*

The demand for qualified parole and probation officers is especially great in large metropolitan areas. The field is open to women and all minorities. Some officers advance by acquiring additional education that qualifies them for positions in other areas of law enforcement.

*Requirements*

When a position is open, a job announcement is prepared. The announcement contains everything an applicant needs to know about the job, including title, duties, and salary. It describes the work, the location, the education and experience requirements, the kind of exam to be given, and the system of rating. It states which application form is to be filled out and where and when to file it.

The following are places where information about careers in probation and parole can be obtained.

- The offices of the State Employment Service. (You can find the address of the one nearest you in the telephone directory.)
- The state Civil Service Commission. (Address your inquiry to the capital city of your state.)
- The city Civil Service Commission, Department of Personnel.
- The municipal building and the library.
- The newspaper. (Many newspapers run a section on regional Civil Service news.)

*Income*

Probation and parole officers earn from $16,000 to $25,000 a year.

*Additional Sources of Information*

American Correctional Association
4321 Hartwick Road
College Park, MD 20740

Association of Paroling Authorities
Sam Houston University
Huntsville, TX 77341

Parole Officers Survey
Corrections Compendium
Contact Center, Inc.
P.O. Box 81826
Lincoln, NE 68501

# Chapter VIII

# Security Guards

Private security involves the protection of assets, people, property, and data in private industry or the public sector. Private security personnel work as employees of major corporations, government agencies, and contract security companies.

Lives, as well as business survival, often depend on the effectiveness of a guard company. The job is an important one. Security officers are hard-working, dedicated persons who take great pride in their chosen work.

Because of the recent rise in crime rates, businesses and corporations have gone to private patrol agencies for help. As a result there is a need for responsible security officers. These security officers work somewhat like law-enforcement officers, not unlike police officers. Security personnel are paid by private employers, and their powers are defined by law.

The most professional security officers help to protect buildings and facilities. They also help with law-enforcement problems that arise. Their main responsibility is to support and enforce the law and to preserve order. Officers must have the unique ability to look at a given situation and be able to figure out step by step how it came about.

If a guard is stationed in a bank and notices a suspicious character loitering around, he should not let the subject pass without being questioned. The guard should make a note of the person's appearance and detain the person until assured of his right to be where he is. Certain questions should immediately rise in the guard's mind when he or she notices anything out of the ordinary. For example:

- Why does this subject appear nervous when entering a place of business and asking to see a certain employee?
- Why is this person here after hours without an appointment, asking to see the head of a certain department?
- Why is a bank customer asking questions about where money is kept or about inside banking procedures?
- A person's name is not on an admittance list, yet he is demanding entry. What is this person's business, and who should be notified?

Security guards should be able to talk to all kinds of people, of all ages and backgrounds. Most guards admit that they have a feeling for detective work, for at times they must act as policemen or firemen or paramedics or private investigators. Courage is imperative. Many officers agree that the best assignments are those that make them responsible for the protection of people or property against danger.

"I saved a life, and it's something I will never forget. I was working as a guard in a Chicago high-rise back in 1981. A fire broke out on the 18th floor. I saw the smoke on one of my desk monitors, then heard the alarms go off. It looked like it was coming from a back storage room. Something must have happened with the alarms on that floor, because when I looked at my number 3 monitor for that floor, the secretaries were still working at their desks.

"I called up and told them to get off the floor. They started running out to the stairwells, but there was one girl left who I guess was in the restroom. She didn't know what was going on, but when she saw the smoke coming down the hallway, she panicked and ran into her boss's office, which was empty. The fire department hadn't arrived, so I left my station and went up to the 18th floor. I was pounding on the door telling her to open it, but she wouldn't unlock the door. I kicked the door in and pulled her screaming and crying down 17 flights of stairs. When I got back to my station, a crowd started clapping and whistling. They had seen everything on the monitor at my desk, and I was the hero of the day."

Micky, 42

"I work as a guard at the front gate of a stereo manufacturing plant. All parts from shipping and receiving have to be cleared by me. Besides having the responsibility for factory parts, I am also on the lookout for inside employee theft, which does happen.

"In the past three years that I have been working here, I have been threatened, set up, and held up at gunpoint. I once broke up an inside job that had speaker parts going out the door in empty trash barrels. I made enemies of the guys that tried to pull it off, but those kind I don't count as friends anyway. The company was overjoyed. I saved them a bundle of money and got a bonus from the president of the company and from my boss at the security company too. I like working in security. It has its moments, but what job doesn't?"

Patrick, 29

"My job is not that tough, but I enjoy it. I work as a guard at a museum. People always ask me if I want to change jobs with them. They kid around because it seems so easy. I like it because I get to meet people from all over the country. I like children, and since our museum has a separate museum for young people, I am always asked questions about where something is or how something works. I find that people in general are pretty good-natured. A few problems happen on the job, but they are not that serious. Our museum has an elaborate electronic security system, so if anything suspicious happens the police are immediately alerted. My job is mainly to direct people, answer questions as best I can, and make sure that everyone is out and that things are put away for closing time. I'm working here part time and attending classes at the university in preparation for a career in law enforcement. This job is great experience for whatever area of law enforcement I choose to go into in the future."

Karen, 22

The job of security officer does not mean that a person merely sits behind a desk and watches a monitor, or checks incoming and outgoing supplies of a company. Guards must think on their feet. They must always be alert and on the lookout for suspicious characters or circumstances. A guard may be the one to foil a robbery at a bank or stop a kidnapper from taking a newborn baby on a hospital maternity ward. The opportunities in the security field are vast. A guard may be hired to patrol the outside of a building, which would mean making rounds, checking windows and doors, checking alarms and electrical and plumbing systems to make sure that everything is in working order.

At airports, guards are hired to protect merchandise being shipped as well as property and equipment. They screen passengers and visitors for weapons, explosives, and other forbidden articles. Guards make sure that nothing is stolen while being loaded or unloaded and watch for trouble among work crews.

Another area of security is in the surveillance of art galleries or museums, where officers are hired to protect paintings and exhibits. They also answer questions from visitors. At social affairs, sports events, conventions, and other public gatherings, guards maintain order, give information, and watch for persons who might cause trouble.

Guards who patrol often work on foot, but if the property is large they may make their rounds by car or motorcycle. In bars or nightclubs, guards maintain radio contact with other guards who are patrolling another area of the premises. Many guards work as bouncers to keep order among the customers and to protect the property.

Among private security specialties are guarding nuclear plants, hospitals, corporations, banks, campuses, utilities, and motels/hotels.

*Bank Guard*

Guarding banks is a high-profile and somewhat high-pressure job. You must always be alert until the moment you are relieved by another guard. Anything can happen in a split second, and the guard's eyes and ears must always be attuned to the goings-on inside the bank. If you choose this career, be prepared to be asked questions, such as the location of the loan department or the place for credit card applications. You will also have to deal with customers' complaints, from the time it took them to move through the line, to the paintings that hang on the walls. A bank security guard must be courteous and listen patiently to everything.

*Campus Security Officer*

The police department does not have the manpower to supervise many areas of campus property. Guides are hired to patrol traffic on the grounds as well as handle any disturbances that may occur. Because of the large numbers of students massed in one area, it isn't unusual for fights to break out or rowdiness to occur. Campus guards must have patience, tact, and courtesy but not be afraid to use force if necessary to insure the safety of the students and the administration.

*Corporate Security Officer*

One of the best places to obtain good training is the guard force of a corporate or industrial organization. Guards in this field are responsible for overall policing and procedures. They cover such matters as inspection, disaster and emergency preparedness, and employee investigation and clearance.

Corporate security guards are responsible for the control of entrances and exits to the building. The authority to arrest or to search and seize is subject to local police control. Each state, city, and community varies in regulations regarding security.

Corporate security guards usually are supplied with uniforms, badges, and equipment.

This job requires the ability to think and act quickly and to make judgment decisions on the spot. Guards must maintain order and enforce company regulations. They are also expected to watch for fires and suspicious persons and to guard the company against material loss.

## Hospital Security Officer

Hospital guards protect property, prevent crime, watch for fires, and patrol floors. Following are some of the duties of hospital guards:

- Insure safety of personnel leaving or arriving at odd hours.
- Guard against kidnapping of babies on the maternity floor.
- Direct visitors.
- Discourage outside solicitors.
- Handle deliveries of medical supplies and equipment.
- Maintain daily log of activities.

Hospital guards are protective agency employees. They are uniformed and armed.

## Armored Car Guards

Armored car guards protect money and valuables in transit. They are often the target of robberies and therefore are trained in the use of firearms.

Armored car guards must know who remains inside the car and exactly how many paces he/she stands from the person next to him/her. Every move is thought out, planned, and rehearsed. There is even a sequence for reentering the vehicle.

To guarantee a superior security force, strict screening methods are required. Private security companies use careful means to insure that guards are of the highest quality. Their backgrounds are checked, and drug tests are often required.

*Government Guards*

Government guards patrol all types of federal properties throughout the U.S., protecting them, their contents, and their occupants. Guards prevent unauthorized entry to restricted areas and unauthorized removal of property from all areas. They maintain their posts, control traffic, and take immediate action against hazards that may cause damage or injury. Guards also make arrests for cause and write required reports.

The job requires moderate to great physical exertion and sometimes courteous contact with the public. All people are considered for this employment without regard to race, religion, sex, national origin, political affiliation, or any other non-merit factor. Being a veteran is an asset. You must also be mentally and emotionally stable, a citizen of the United States, and eighteen years of age. You must pass a physical exam and a background check.

To apply for this position, obtain a copy of the pamphlet that is published by the U.S. Civil Service Commission.

*How Do You Get a Security Job?*

Many security officers are college-educated, highly professional, and trained in security procedures. They are trained in CPR, basic fighting techniques, and loss-prevention measures. The company that hires a security guard has a right to expect honesty and professionalism.

The protection business is booming. American firms spend some $6 billion a year on contract guard services and an additional $11 billion on in-house guards. About 900,000 private guards are at work in the United States, up 300 percent since 1969, and almost twice the number of state and local police officers. The field has experienced a steady 15 percent annual growth rate over the last fifteen years and is expected to increase accordingly in the future.

If this line of work interests you, there are steps you can take now to prepare. If you have choices of school subjects, try for classes in American history, civics, English, and possibly typing. You will be better prepared to understand federal laws, state statutes, city ordinances, and security material, and to prepare reports that may be read in court.

You may want to take a part-time job that will enable you to get acquainted with security work. Apply for work at sports events such as soccer, baseball, or even wrestling matches. Offer your help to security agencies in jobs such as secretarial, bookkeeping, or vehicle repair that might acquaint you with the field.

Once you have made the decision to work as a security guard, be prepared to have your life checked out, from the date of your birth to the time of your application. Investigation will be made into your credit rating, your education, past employment, medical history, and service records. You will take courses in the responsibility of security personnel, in criminal law, court procedures, first aid, investigations and protection, crowd control, and handling of firearms.

Applicants are expected to have good character references, no police record, and good health, especially in hearing and vision. Most employers prefer high school graduates, but applicants with less education can qualify if they pass reading and writing tests and demonstrate competence in following written and oral instructions. Some jobs require a driver's permit. Employers also seek people with experience in the military police or in state and local police departments.

Security officers must be able to read and write English. You must be a citizen of the United States. You must be able to follow written and spoken orders and think and act without panic in emergencies. You will be fingerprinted, and the prints will be sent to the FBI in Washington and to the police departments of cities where you have lived.

You may have to be bonded, meaning that someone guarantees to make good any damage or loss caused by an action of yours.

*Women in Security*

Women security guards are employed in all areas. They are used in surveillance, as security in public assemblies, sports events, industrial plants, and hospitals. Female security officers are a part of every protection agency's staff.

*Minorities*

All minorities are encouraged to apply for positions in security. The International Organization of Black Security Executives (IOBSE) is dedicated to promoting opportunities in security management for minorities. It is a nonprofit organization that shares expertise and information regarding security jobs throughout the nation. Each year members put on programs at black colleges and universities to inform students about private security careers. For further information on the IOBSE, write to the treasurer:

Kerry V. Scott
P.O. Box 594
Columbia, MD 21045

*Salaries*

Depending on their experience, in1988 newly hired guards in the federal government earned between $12,000 and $14,000 a year. Private security guards earn between $11,000 and $25,000 a year, depending on if you are just starting out or working in security administration. Jobs vary and some companies pay more than others. Although guards in smaller private companies receive periodic salary increases, advancement is likely to be limited. Most large organizations, however, use a military type of ranking that offers advancement in position and salary. In-house guards enjoy higher earnings and benefits, greater job security, and more advancement potential than contract security guards. They are usually given more training and responsibility.

Guard experience enables some persons to transfer to police jobs that offer higher pay and greater opportunities for advancement.

Guards with some college education may advance to jobs that involve administrative duties of the prevention of espionage or sabotage. A few guards with management skills open their own contract security agencies.

*Job Outlook*

Job openings for guards are expected to be plentiful through the year 2000. High turnover in this occupation ranks it among those providing the greatest number of job openings in the entire economy.

*Related Occupations*

Occupations related to security guard include bailiff, border guard, corrections officer, deputy sheriff, fish and game warden, house or store detective, police officer, and private investigator.

*Sources of Additional Information*

Further information about work opportunities for guards is available from local employers and from the State Employment Service. Information about registration and licensing requirements for guards may be obtained from the state Licensing Commission or the state Police Department.

For information about federal contract guard job requirements, write for:

Contract Guard Information Manual
(GPO Publication 022-00-00192-2)
U.S. Government Printing Office
Washington, DC 20402

The following is an interview with a security officer who is currently working in Los Angeles, California.

My name is Mario, I am 55 years old, and I work in security at one of the major movie studios.

Q: Can you describe your duties?

A: They vary. I oversee and supervise the guards at their respective gates, I do on-site investigations of accidents that occur on the set, and I oversee safety and security procedures at the studio.

Q: Do you feel that this is a rewarding or challenging job at this point in your career?

A: Yes, it is.

Q: In what way?

A: It goes beyond the simple situation of the guard sitting at the gate and checking who goes in and who goes out. I am now involved in the administrative aspect of the job, which determines policies and procedures to avoid any hazardous situations on the lot.

Q: While you have been working at the studio, have you ever had occasion to draw your gun, or have you found yourself in a dangerous situation?

A: We in the security staff on the set do not carry guns.

Q: Can you remember a time when you felt that you had to rise to the occasion, so to speak?

A: There are times, usually when there is a union problem that results in pickets about the studio lot. Usually some people try to keep others from entering the lot, and that does get difficult to handle, because tempers flare and I have conflicting interests. One is trying to control the ongoing operations of the lot, and the other is trying to keep the strike situation under control. Sometimes very heated arguments transpire.

Q: Before you came to work at the studio, what were your earlier jobs as a guard?

A: After leaving high school, I was offered a job as a bouncer at a nightclub in Anaheim. It consisted of checking out IDs, making sure that the staff was adequately protected, and making sure that no problems occurred inside or outside the establishment. After that I began to get interested in security, in the procedures and such. After a short time I was elevated to chief doorman and stayed in that position for two and a half years. I obtained my guard's license and the appropriate baton and mace licenses. From there I got a job at a studio from contacts that I made in the entertainment industry. I provided security at the lounge. Not long after I heard of an opening at a studio near my home, and I jumped at the chance. I worked hard and was able to advance to different positions within the studio to the point where I am now, advisor on all policy and procedures. I have a staff of twelve beneath me.

Q: Is there any advice you can give young adults who are interested in entering the field of security?

A: Anyone intending to enter the security field should remember first and most important to have a *clean record*. That includes staying clear of drugs and any other unlawful activity. This will be thoroughly checked by any employer looking for security personnel. Second, you must have the proper training. A number of schools are available. Attend a reputable school, obtain your baton license, your mace license, and if you are interested in a job within a particular company, find out their requirements and satisfy those requirements before you apply. That way, you are almost assured of landing a job over someone who has to start fullfilling the requirements you have already completed.

Q: What is your opinion on future opportunities for security jobs?

A: There will always be opportunities for security guards. They have a tendency to be somewhat transitory and therefore there is a higher than average replacement factor. Normally, applicants start working as guards, then become supervisors, then advance to directors of security at different companies. When they reach that point they find that it is a very comfortable job; it is a fun job because there are always new and different situations facing you.

Q:   On a final note, as a top man in the security field, what would you look for in hiring a person for a job?

A:   I would look for a clean appearance and a clean record, along with a desire to succeed in the job.

*Chapter* **IX**

---

# Private Investigator

Private investigators perform a wide variety of duties. They work for insurance companies, law firms, and private individuals. The life of a private investigator can be exciting. Many investigators own their own business and employ a staff such as a secretary and an assistant to help in the search for documents and to deliver court records to attorneys and businesses.

Usually a great deal of travel is involved in this profession. You may be called upon to locate a witness and bring him in for an upcoming trial, or to perform a sub rosa investigation, that is, to watch a person without that person's knowledge.

*Insurance Company Investigator*

Perhaps a person is claiming injury to his back. He slipped and fell at a restaurant and is making a claim for compensation to the restaurant's insurance company. Not only is he looking to be paid for his injury, but also to be reimbursed for the days he had to take off work and for a housekeeper he had to hire to make his meals and take care of him while he was home in bed.

The investigator is called in and asked to check out the facts before any money is paid. The insurance company wants to know how exactly the person fell, what were the contributing factors to the fall, whether the person had a bad back to begin with, and many more details. It wants to determine its liability.

The first thing an investigator does when he receives an

## ASSIGNMENT SHEET

DATE REC'D:  August 3, 1989        FROM:  Samantha R. Robbins
                                   OF:    American Casualty
                                          Insurance Co.

CLAIM #    POLICY #        EFFECTIVE DATES      OTHER
750613     RSR658000       5/7/88 to 5/7/89

INSURED:    Marty's Restaurant    INSURED'S ATTY:    No attorney
            343 North Main St.                       involved
            Minneapolis,
            Minnesota
     Tel:   612/555-0907                    Tel:

CLAIMANT:   Joseph Skinner        CLAIMANT'S ATTY:   No attorney
            21356 E. 22nd St.                        involved
            Minneapolis,
            Minn. 55406
     Tel:                                    Tel:

DATE OF LOSS:   12/22/88          TYPE OF LOSS:   Slip and Fall

INCIDENT DESCRIPTION:   Joseph Skinner entered Marty's Restaurant at 11:30 a.m. on December 12, 1988. He claims to have slipped on water that was left on the floor in front of the salad bar area. Subject alleges he fell, landing on his back, and sustained injury to his upper and middle back. Paramedics arrived and subject was transported to Northfield Hospital, where he was treated and released.

NEEDS/INSTRUCTIONS:      (X) FULL INVESTIGATION

COMMENTS:(If Any)   Find out what substance was on the floor area at time of fall; investigate clean-up procedures for restaurant; ask for hospital bills along with any other applicable medical receipts.

1)   Obtain J. Skinner statement     4)   Photos of restaurant floor
2)   Witness statements (if any)     5)   Obtain medical reports
3)   Statement from Manager          6)   Obtain wage loss statement

assignment is to meet with the person who is hiring his services. He brings with him an Assignment Sheet and asks questions to clarify his duties in performing the investigation. He wants the names of the parties; the names of any witnesses; the date of the incident; and a statement from the personnel of the restaurant.

After the investigator has all the information needed, he/she makes a call to the person making the claim—provided the subject has not retained an attorney. If there is an attorney, he or she will deal directly with the insurance company and the investigator, and no contact will be permitted with the claimant.

The investigator and the claimant set a time and place for an interview. The investigator usually brings a camera to photograph a visible injury or the accident area. A tape recorder is used, and a question/answer type of interview takes place. The investigator knows that he/she must research the incident, asking many questions to help determine liability. A complete picture must be brought forth, including times, dates, names, and places. In this back injury case, the investigator will ask:

- What were the weather conditions on the day of the accident?
- What kind of shoes was the subject wearing when he slipped and fell?
- Was the subject on any type of medication that may have caused him to be off-balance?
- Were there any warning signs about the condition of the floor on the day in question?

Once the facts have been determined, the investigator writes a report to the insurance company. The tape-recorded statement is transcribed by the secretary or an outside typing service. The photographs are developed and mounted on a photo sheet. Diagrams are included, as well as the investigator's comments on the facts surrounding the claim. An activity log is filled in, showing the work the investigator has performed. The

| DATE | ACTIVITY LOG | EXPENSES | TIME |
|------|-------------|----------|------|
| 1/7/89 | Received file information, called J. | | |
| | Skinner and made appointment for | | |
| | statement and photos of his injury. | | .3 |
| 1/11/89 | Met with J. Skinner, obtained statement | | |
| | regarding fall at restaurant. Obtained | | |
| | medical reports and additional misc. bills. | | 2.0 |
| 1/13/89 | Called Marty's Restaurant, spoke with | | |
| | manager, Ron Miller. Made arrangements | | |
| | to inspect area and speak to clean-up | | |
| | personnel. | | .2 |
| 1/15/89 | Drove to Marty's Restaurant, spoke to | | |
| | Ron Miller and cashier who was witness to | | |
| | incident. Obtained statement from Miller | | |
| | and cashier Sarah Downey. Photographed | | |
| | floor area. | | 2.5 |
| 1/19/89 | Firest report to insurance company | | |
| | regarding findings to date. | | .5 |
| | | Total Hours... | 5.5 |

PHOTO SHEET

OWNER   Bradford Investigations     IDENTIFICATION NUMBER   CIC 600
LOCATION   Marty's Restaurant
COMPANY CLAIM NUMBER   750613       POLICY NUMBER   RSR65800
FILM   35MM   POLAROID ☐   NEGATIVE ☐   DATE TAKEN   1/6/88

PICTURE # 1
DESCRIPTION

Subject J. Skinner
bruises to middle
and lower back

PICTURE # 2
DESCRIPTION

Inside floor
area of Marty's
Restaurant
Location of
claimant's fall

complete file is copied, and the original is sent to the insurance company, usually within thirty days.

*Missing Persons Search*

A private investigator may be hired by persons to locate missing family members. The fee is agreed upon before any work is initiated. An investigator's fee to locate a person can be as little as $10 to $15 an hour plus expenses or as much as $200 or more.

A private investigator hired to find a missing person is virtually on call. Phone calls come in at all hours of the day and night. People that the investigator speaks to during the day may remember additional information and want to relate it as soon as possible. A great deal of travel is involved in the locating of missing persons. One investigator explains:

> "When I am asked to find someone, I use every available source of information that comes my way. This includes clues that family members drop in the course of a conversation, or recollections of a missing person's past activities, something that may lead me to their present whereabouts.
>
> "I also use information from the Department of Motor Vehicles, real estate information, and from the subject's past employers or neighbors.
>
> "When I do locate a missing person, I ask the person who hired me what he wants to do. I never take it upon myself to apprehend a person. If I am asked to serve a subpoena, I will. At times I will call in a policeman or the marshal to accompany me to the door. This is when I know I will be met with hostility and I feel the situation might be dangerous.
>
> "Each of my cases is different. I feel a sense of satisfaction when I have found a loved one, a friend, or a family member. I like to see people reunited in a happy way. I know I have done my job."
>
> Ed, 45

The following is an interview with Paul Cohen, coauthor and owner of Cohen & Associates.

Q. Paul, can you describe a typical day for a private investigator?

A. One has to understand that a day in the life of a private investigator is far from typical. It is different from morning to morning. The day usually begins earlier than everyone else's and ends later than most. Normally, one has to get to the office and start on the paperwork. By that I mean that you have to keep up with the daily reporting to whoever gave you the assignments, your principals, so that they will be informed as to how the case or claim is progressing. Without that, your usefulness as a private investigator is limited.

Once the paperwork and dictation of reports is completed, the day must be planned. The plan may consist of outlining the items to be done during the day on the cases, or it may just be a geographic outline of the areas to which you must travel and the times of your appointments. You need to coordinate the times and places to maximize the value of the day.

When the regular day is over, an investigator checks in with his or her answering service or secretary and gets the day's messages. The calls will be returned and the needs or requests of the callers taken care of. The investigator then tries to complete appointments that he/she was unable to take care of during the day. That may include talking to witnesses who can meet only after working hours. The day of a busy investigator can start as early as 7:00 a.m. and end as late as midnight.

Q. What are some of the rewards of working as a P.I.?

A. The first, in my opinion, is the financial reward. An average investigator in the United States can earn in excess of $35 an hour plus time and expenses. That can add up to about $50 or $55 an hour. Some investigators charge up to $100 an hour.

Besides the financial rewards, the most rewarding aspect of this job is that I am able to find out the truth without concern for any liability determination. My job as an investigator is to determine once and for all what the true facts are. It is irrelevant whether the facts are in favor of one person or another. I derive great personal satisfaction in knowing the truth, as opposed to who is at fault or who is responsible.

I like being out and around during the day. I find sitting behind a desk all day somewhat confining and restricting. Some people, and I guess I'm one of them, find that they are unable to sit behind a desk and work in accounting or inventory control, seeing the same paperwork and the same people throughout the day. In my job I may never see the same individual or the same claim in a pile of 200 that I am asked to investigate. The facts may be similar, but the personalities I meet vary from day to day. That keeps me enthusiastic about the job, in high spirits, and always looking forward to the next case.

Q.   What are some drawbacks or dangers of the job?

A.   Well, it is very time-consuming and very stressful. There are limits on the number of cases that you can perform competently. Many investigators take on numerous cases but do not give each case the careful attention it deserves. Others take on too few and give them total attention, but find out that the money runs short and they cannot make an adequate living. A good investigator tries to pace the caseload and plan the work accordingly.

A danger of the job is that it sometimes puts you in unusual situations. If you approach a person with the intention of getting facts for a case, the person may be angry about the case and vent his or her anger or frustration on you. For example, you might be hired to investigate an automobile accident. You may be met with anger and hostility because you represent a law firm or an insurance company, and the parties see you as an enemy.

Another area that may involve danger is process serving, the serving of documents from a law office or court requiring a person's presence for trial or for a deposition. Process serving is usually done by people who are just starting out in the field and may need the hours of work to qualify for a license. On the other hand, it may be done by very experienced people who have a knack for finding people and are hired specifically for the purpose. In my opinion, not a great deal of money is to be made by limiting oneself to process serving. Also, people value their privacy, and when a stranger comes to door and tries to serve them with papers—especially if the case involves anger—the process server immediately becomes the enemy.

Q.   Can you explain the "sub rosa" part of investigating?

A.   That situation arises when attorneys deal with each other in the handling of a lawsuit. When opposing sides, plaintiff and defendant's attorneys, set out to determine who is liable for an accident or injury, the need arises to determine the exact extent of the injury sustained.

An investigator is hired to observe the injured party without his being aware of the surveillance. The procedure is allowed by law, as long as one does not interrupt, interfere, or cause any nuisance to the person. A sub rosa investigation allows the investigator to see the person bowling when he claims he is bedridden with a sprained back, watch him mow his lawn although he claims he is in a wheelchair with a broken leg, or playing baseball even though he is making a claim for a sprained arm. The investigator is not allowed to climb the fence or peer through the windows.

In a sub rosa investigation you determine where the person resides, where he works, and what his outside activities are. You may take photographs. If you find a major discrepancy, you put it in your report.

Q.   What resources do you use to assist in tracking down missing persons?

A.   My office does not do a great deal of missing-persons work, but often when I am called upon to produce a witness, the task becomes finding him or her. One has to realize that the process of litigation may take up to four years. The people involved in a case have a tendency to move around. They become lost in the sense that addresses are no longer applicable, some have moved to different states, phone numbers have been changed.

Unless the investigator can secure information such as a social security number or the name and address of a family member, it can become very difficult to find a person who has moved. My office gets numerous calls from attorneys who need a witness immediately but can't find him. My first move would be to check with the Department of Motor Vehicles to locate an auto registration. I would check the voters' registration, the public library for old phone books, fictitious business filings, criminal cases in the event that the person is in prison. I would check with family members, with the post office, and with neighbors.

Services are being established whereby one can search data bases. These enable an investigator to search for information in the comfort of his office. The services are still limited, however, and can be costly.

Q. Do you feel there will be a demand for private investigators in the future?

A. At the rate litigation is increasing in the United States, I feel that the number of competent investigators will rise. There is a great need for licensed private investigators in the Western states. I can only speak for this part of the country.

Q. What background or skills would one need for a career in the investigation field?

A. Requirements vary from state to state. One has to prove to the state Department of Consumer Affairs that he has put in sufficient hours working for another licensed private investigator or in the investigation field. California requires that the hours total 6,000 and be under the direct supervision of an investigator or an attorney. The hours can include working in a law office or performing duties associated with a claim. After accumulating enough hours, you must take and pass a state exam.

If someone was serious about working for a license, I

would recommend that he contact a licensed investigator and introduce himself. Let the investigator know that you are interested in working as an assistant to learn the business. Leave your name and phone number, and perhaps send a résumé of your past work or experience.

Q.  What advice would you give a student or young adult thinking about entering this line of work?

A.  I suggest strongly that you complete a four-year college degree, with a major in some related area such as business management or an area where your inquisitive skills would be heightened. By this I mean science, biology, police science, or other related courses. Any area that would require you to ask WHY? WHY did this occur? WHY is this being done? Other than that, you can choose a part-time job that will introduce you to various areas of law or investigation, such as researching, law clerking, even working as a runner delivering papers from the courthouse to law offices.

A number of schools promise to make you a detective in three hours or three days at the John Doe Academy of Private Investigators. Some reputable courses are available, but beware of the ones that offer you the world in an overnight package. They may teach you the fundamentals of investigatory work, but they have a poor record of placing people in licensed investigation firms. In my opinion, assisting a licensed investigator in his day-to-day business, taking notes, and asking questions will help you more than just reading a book about how it is done. The field is interesting, rewarding, and a great career choice.

*Applying for the Job*

Perhaps after reading the preceding interview you feel that this career sounds interesting. What next? Start by looking in the newspaper for openings as an investigator's assistant. The ad would probably read something like this:

*ASSIST PRIVATE INVESTIGATOR*
Locate court records, write reports,
assist P.I. in running of business.
Must have car with insurance.
Contact Ann
after 3:00 p.m.

Following are some things the authors look for when hiring an employee to assist them in their investigation business.

- Does the applicant appear to have the emotional balance necessary for the job? Does he/she appear to be in control, or seem as though he would come apart under stress?
- Does the applicant appear to have a real interest in working as an investigator? (We often come across people who apply just for the fun of it, for something to do to fill their time. They have no real interest in the job, and it shows in their work performance.)
- Does the applicant appear serious-minded and intelligent? Will he/she be able to weigh the merits of a question before deciding, or will he/she make a snap judgment?
- Does he/she show confidence and self-reliance?
- Will the applicant be able to grasp ideas quickly?
- Does the applicant have positive references from past employers or from people in the community who can give a character reference?
- Does he/she have good manners and a pleasant personality? (We always keep in mind that our employees are a reflection of ourselves and our office. A neat and courteous staff is a reflection of a professional business office.)

*Experience*

Many related jobs can qualify as experience in working toward an investigator's license. Work in library research helps with researching court records and documents. The ability to drive the streets of your city and know how to get from place to place is a plus. It is important to be able to speak with other people in a knowledgeable and polite manner, such as court clerks, legal secretaries, store managers, etc.

It is a sure bet that an investigation firm will hire a less experienced but enthusiastic person over one who has many credits but has a lethargic of personality. Investigators come from all walks of life. Students, housewives, and grandmothers have earned the necessary hours to become licensed investigators. After you accumulate your hours, you write to the Department of Consumer Affairs in your state asking for a license application. They will send you an information packet and instructions. Most states require that you pass an exam. Following is the form used by the state of Minnesota for a private detective license. Again, each state varies, so it is advisable to contact your state board to determine what exactly you will need to obtain your license.

## STATE OF MINNESOTA

Private Detective and Protective Agent Services Board
1246 University Avenue
St. Paul, MN 55104
(612)642-0775

### *APPLICATION REQUIREMENTS/PROCEDURES*

The licensing requirements and procedures for Private Detectives and Protective Agents are defined in Minnesota State Statutes 326.32 to 326.339. This information sheet summarizes the key requirements and procedures involved. For specific language, refer directly to the statutes.

Definitions regarding the application process can be found in the introductory portion of the statute. Specifically, for identification purposes, the following positions will require that distinctions be made:

*APPLICANT*—Any individual making application for a private detective or protective agent license on an individual license level.

*QUALIFIED REPRESENTATIVE*—Refers to the individual to be involved in the day to day management and supervision of the licensed activity in a partnership or corporation. This subject is required to meet all qualification standards as dictated by statute.

*MINNESOTA MANAGER*—If a license applicant is a partnership or corporation, based outside Minnesota, it will require the designation of a Minnesota Manager for any business regularly conducted at a Minnesota office location. The candidate for this position is required to meet the same experience qualifications as the Qualified Representative.

As an introduction to the statute the following are some of the basic requirements of applicants, qualified representatives, Minnesota managers, and those parties signing the application:

1. Each person signing the application must be at least 18 years of age.
2. Each person must have a record free of felony convictions, and no record of convictions of offenses stipulated in statute.
3. Each license applicant must supply a $10,000 Surety Bond (private detective or protective agent) at the time of application.
4. Each license applicant must supply Proof of Financial Responsibility (options for fulfillment are delineated in statute) at the time of application.
5. Complete required application materials and supporting documents.
6. Be of good character, honesty and integrity.

*EXPERIENCE*—The applicant, qualified representative or Minnesota manager for a PRIVATE DETECTIVE license must provide documentation supporting a minimum of 6,000 hours of employment, as an investigator in one or more of the following areas, showing competancy and ability:

1. Employed as an investigator with a licensed private detective agency.
2. Employed as an investigator with a United States government investigative service.
3. Employed as an investigator for a city police department or sheriff's office.
4. Be employed in an occupation that the Board would find to be equivalent in scope, responsibility and training as one of the specific occupations listed above.

Each of the above qualification areas must be in line with dictates of Board rules.

*EXPERIENCE*—The applicant, qualified representative or Minnesota manager for a PROTECTIVE AGENT license must provide documentation supporting a minimum of 6,000 hours of employment in one or more of the following areas, showing competency and ability:

1. Employed in a protective/security capacity with a licensed protective agent, or in a protective/security, or investigative capacity for a licensed private detective. Subject is to have demonstrated experience in security systems, audits and supervision.
2. Employed in a protective/security capacity or as an investigator with a United States government investigative service.
3. Employed in a protective/security capacity, or as an investigator with a city police department or sheriff's office.
4. Be employed in an occupation that the Board would find upon review to be equivalent in scope, responsibility and training to one of the specific occupations listed above.

Each of the above qualification areas must be in line with dictates of Board rules.

The application package is provided by the Board once requested, and it first determined which license is being applied for, and what level of license is being sought (individual, partnership or corporation).

Minnesota statute outlines an application and qualification process for licensing. There is no testing requirement presently included in this process. Once an application package has been received, a required 20 day posting period occurs. This is a public announcement that a particular individual or business has made application.

*Each person signing the application (i.e. Qualified Representative, Applicant, Minnesota Manager, Chief Executive Officer, Chief Financial Officer, Partner) must comply with the following:*

1. Complete appropriate application forms (with appropriate signatures).
2. Complete a criminal history request form.
3. Submit a recent photograph and a full set of fingerprints.
4. Provide five references (not related by blood or marriage) who have known the subject for a minimum of five years.

Additionally then the Qualified Representative and/or Minnesota Manager must provide documentation of work experience (as outlined).

The application must also be accompanied by the noted $10,000 Surety Bond and Proof Financial Responsibility.

Once completed, an application should be submitted to the Board's administrative office at:

1246 University Avenue
St. Paul, MN 55104

Any questions can be addressed to the Board's Director, Marie Ohman at (612) 642-0775.

## *LICENSE FEE SCHEDULE*

All applications must be accompanied by a nonrefundable application fee of $15.00.

License Fees are as follows:

**PRIVATE DETECTIVE:**
| | |
|---|---|
| Individual | $500.00 |
| Partnership | $850.00 |
| Corporation | $950.00 |

**PROTECTIVE AGENT:**
| | |
|---|---|
| Individual | $400.00 |
| Partnership | $800.00 |
| Corporation | $900.00 |

*In the event that an application for license is denied, one-half of the initial license fee will be refunded.

All checks or money orders should be made payable to the "Private Detective and Protective Agent Services Board."

# Chapter X

# Beyond the Badge

This chapter comprises comments by ordinary people in the field of law enforcement and security—and their families.

"My dad was on the force for six years. At the end before he left, he was really stressed out. I remember one Christmas day in 1986 there was a shoot-out at a gas station downtown. His partner was shot and killed by a guy who robbed the place of $44. The killing was senseless, and Dad never got over it. His partner was also his best friend.

"I know the cops expect the worst to happen when they walk in to break up a roberry or murder attempt. They're prepared for it. But I don't think anyone is ever prepared when the worst actually happens. It takes everyone by surprise and leaves scars that last forever."

"I've been in traffic enforcement about three years now. It's a good job, and I like my work. I deal with ticketing vehicles for sign violations and meters and zone-stopping. I also oversee tow-away warnings.

"I've heard just about every excuse in the book. Older women have propositioned me to get out of a ticket. I've seen grown men cry. I've been threatened, lied to, and offered bribes. Sometimes I wonder, you know, it's only a ticket. But the stories that people come up with never cease to amaze me."

"Drug trafficking is not done out in the open. When dealers are out selling, they usually hide the stash somewhere and keep small amounts on them. That way if they get caught, the case usually won't go through the courts. It's tough, because I know what the real story is. I'm on to their activities. But the burden of proof is on me, and sometimes those dealers are let off free because there is a lack of evidence. Sometimes you get lucky and sometimes you don't."

"When I started at the police academy, I was proud that I had made it through the hiring process to become a police officer. I finally earned the needed credits, and my application was accepted. I took and passed the exam. The past few years have been good ones. I have many friends on the force and have been able to serve on different jobs in our community.

"There was a time when I thought the job was too much for me. I was involved in a heavy arrest situation and was shot twice in the right shoulder. I was ready to walk away, but later I learned that the guy I eventually arrested had been terrorizing kids. I received thank-yous from lots of people for helping to put the guy away. I guess in each of us there is something that keeps us going as cops."

"In my eight years with the New York police I have worked on a number of different assignments. The ones that get to me the most are the domestic violence calls. I may spend three hours trying to settle a fight where a boyfriend has bloodied his girlfriend's face. Black eyes, broken nose, the works. The time I spend is not getting him away from her, but trying to persuade her to press charges. She's afraid of what might happen to him and she's trying to protect him. After all he's done to her, it ends up being me that they're mad at. I sometimes wonder what makes people think and act the way they do. I can handle drug arrests and homicides and the worst of cases, but getting involved in domestic disputes is to me the toughest part of this job."

"My wife works vice in the Miami district. I worry about her because of all the crazies out there. She sometimes works as a decoy in the worst parts of town, you know, trying to flush the bad guys out of their hiding places. Pimps and prostitutes approach her, and she makes arrests on the spot. She gets involved in drug busts and has many close calls.

"Even though her job puts her in dangerous positions, she says she loves the work. She says that she never knows when a routine assignment will turn into an exciting challenge. She loves getting the bad guys. I have to admit that I'm proud of my wife. I worry about her all the time, but the honors she has received and the respect she has from her colleagues make me feel that she's really doing her job, and a good one at that."

"I work as a police diver. My specialty is retrieving bodies that for one reason or another have ended up at the bottom of a body of water. The work is different and can sometimes be gruesome.

"I've had to search for murder victims whose bodies have been under water for weeks. The ocean diving is the easiest, I think. Swamps are the worst. In swamps, my enemies are alligators and snakes. In the ocean it's the sharks. Our lakes are simple to work in, but the pollution is getting worse each year. I feel that I really earn my pay."

"My husband, Gary, was a Highway Patrol man back in Missouri. We've been divorced for years, but sometimes it seems like yesterday. The first thing I want to say is that I was married to an officer who had a lot of integrity. That I was proud of. I know that he never took a bribe, he never took anything under the table. It happens a lot, but I would like to credit the people who are honest.

"Gary and I raised dogs, bloodhounds. They were ours, but they were also used by the Patrol. On Thanksgiving one year we got a phone call from a woman who was missing her husband. He had been gone forty-eight hours, and they found his car out in the woods. We were just about to sit down to a big dinner, but Gary left immediately and went out with the bloodhounds.

As it turned out, the woman's husband happened to change cars. He got into another car with a woman he had been seeing. When those things happen you get angry. You think, Gee—it should have been something important."

Emil Soorani is a board-certified psychiatrist in Santa Monica, California. He writes:

"I have been working with law enforcement officers from various walks of life—the regular police officer, the deputy sheriff, Secret Service, and parole officers. Even prison guards. My practice is medical/legal, and I work with affective disorders. I get referrals of injured police officers—some injured physically, others chemically.

"The stresses in police work are manifold. One is the bureaucratic stress created by the hierarchy of the police department. Police departments are answerable to cities; cities have changes in administration that put pressure on the chiefs; chiefs put pressure on the captains, who put pressure on the men. And these pressures, that sometimes do not make sense, filter down to the men and women, and they feel it. Pressure in negotiating contracts is stressful. Sometimes the officers involved in negotiations are really harassed.

"One of my former patients had to leave the area and move to a different town. He was able to maintain his rank, but he became the enemy of the city. Sometimes the administrative pressure is as great or greater than the pressure out on the street.

"The beat officers have various pressures: boredom, threats to life, shootings, and witnessing other people's death in car accidents, homicides, and suicides.

"The memory of these incidents cannot escape the officer, it keeps working at the defenses. At some point or other the officer may crack, depending on how much stress he or she has been exposed to over the years.

"Often it is the family that becomes seriously affected by

the stress that the officer brings home. The officer may have trouble sleeping, or become distant. Some try to escape pressure by drinking or having an affair.

"There is often a sense of peer pressure when it comes to drinking: If you don't drink you are not one of the guys or gals.

"Many officers like the respect and the power that come with the job. You do have a lot of power, but as with physicians, people expect too much of you and you expect too much of yourself. You start expecting that you should be a superman, but we all have our limits. We get tired, and officers are exposed to too many deaths, too many dead children. Dead children especially take a great toll on police officers. Overexposure to these situations can cause the officer to develop a chronic post-traumatic stress disorder. All of us need to ignore and suppress the fact that we are going to die, but if you are continuously exposed to it you begin to realize your vulnerability, your mortality. Thus, all kinds of symptoms of post-traumatic stress disorder come into play.

"It may take just one instance, or it may take years. The smarter police officers come forward and say that something is going on; the ones who are more guarded will hide it until they crack up.

"The police departments and the sheriff's departments have psychology departments, but they have their shortcomings. Many men and women fear that the psychologists and psychiatrists working for the department cannot be trusted. Counselors from the outside are more trusted. The men and women feel more comfortable with them because they feel they can open up a little more. I may tell them to retire, but I can do so without their feeling threatened: I'm not doing it to fire them, I'm doing it to help.

"I also work with Secret Service people, many of whom are former cops. The ones who are chosen for Secret Service are really tough, very bright people, men and women, high functioning, high I.Q., good record, very tough people.

"There is a lot of stress, many hours of work, a lot of traveling. They experience marital problems, separation from their families, moving around, a lot of glamour. There is also the outside chance to have an affair.

"I work with law enforcement officers who have problems, both alcohol and depression problems. Many times depression is not recognized until it is very late. I like to work with these guys, to help and lecture in this area. I have been working with police officers from almost every single department since 1982."

*Chapter* **XI**

# Planning Your Career

In previous chapters we talked about the many opportunities available within the law-enforcement and security field.
After reading about the requirements and qualifications that
each job entails, you should have a better understanding
of how and where you should begin to make the necessary
preparations.

Most jobs in this field require that you take courses that will
familiarize you with the work. You can begin by taking high
school elective courses such as civics or political science. You
will also be required to go through a training period, pass a
written or oral examination, or both.

The more specialized careers, such as FBI and Secret Service, require more before you are even considered for the
job. Investigators will dig deep into your background and look
closely at all aspects of your past and present life. Besides
honesty and a desire to work, they will be looking for a law-
abiding citizen with a clear record.

Employers are continuously on the lookout for hard-working,
trustworthy individuals who have a strong desire to succeed in
the job. A good employee is a reflection upon the company or
organization that hires him/her.

Perhaps you have always wanted to become a police officer.
You remember dreaming of wearing a badge and uniform and
proudly serving on the force. Now, as you're approaching
the middle or upper grades of school, the time to make that
decision is growing closer. As you near graduation, a definite
plan of action must be initiated. There are courses to sign up

for and applications to fill out. There are interviews to go on and new people to meet. You must start thinking about your plans for the future and what direction to take.

Listen closely to the advice from those who contributed to this book. Try to remember what was said about police work; about security guards and detectives. Security guards do face some degree of danger in their job, and Secret Service agents often spend a great deal of time traveling and away from their families. But as most who are working in law enforcement and security agree, the rewards far outweigh the drawbacks. If you choose this career you will be responsible for protecting society against thieves, criminals, and other undesirables wishing to harm others. Some of you will be credited with saving lives.

Think how it must feel to be prepared to give up your own life to protect the President of the United States. Or to find a missing child and bring her back to a grateful family. You may be the one who saves a company millions of dollars because of your watchful eye.

The field of law enforcement and security is an important and gratifying career choice, one that has many opportunities just waiting for the right people. Perhaps you are that person. Start by choosing a field that interests you and read all the information you can find about it. Talk to people who are already working in the job. It is never too early to start preparing.

Rudolf Kies, PhD, is a former intelligence officer. He worked as a criminal investigator and was once a deputy sheriff in Lincoln, Nebraska. Kies served as a consultant to local, national, and international investigative agencies throughout the years. Currently he is Director of Kies Intelligence Agency. The authors asked Mr. Kies to contribute his thoughts and feelings about working in the law-enforcement field, and he wrote the following:

*A Career in Law Enforcement*

"Of course, as law enforcement goes, unless one spends a number of years in this type of work, it is extremely difficult to picture or predict a life-style involved with the darker side of human nature. Or is it the darker side?

"We all commit crimes. As one criminal justice professor once put it, we cheat—well, just a little—on taxes, we run an occasional red light, we should put some money in that parking meter from time to time, and so on. But that doesn't make me a criminal, you say. And you are right, it doesn't. Still, the percentage of people with a 'criminal mind' is very low in our society today, thanks to good law enforcement and good social teaching.

"'But then what's the point,' you lament, 'if I can't become a cop and chase real criminals and feel the thrill of the danger involved in this type of work?' Well, in some areas around the country there isn't any work involved in being a cop, or so it seems. But don't forget, chasing criminals is only half of the picture. The other half, of course, is helping people in a plain old-fashioned way. How? Well, if you're a young man thinking of becoming a police officer, think back to when you were a little toddler crossing the street or looking for your dog or riding your bicycle the wrong way.

"You may say 'Gosh, that's not what I want! That's stupid!' Not at all. Police work is an education in itself, and it will take you as far as your ability allows you to go. It is perhaps the only professional field that allows one to enter as a young man, attend some police academy, and after a while continue to improve your education and work performance and 'work your way up.'

"The difficult part in planning one's career, of course, is to know ahead of time just what to expect of oneself, say, ten, twenty years down the road. To attend college and take all the Administration of Justice courses available is a sure way to find recognition in law enforcement. On the other hand, police work is composed of many specialties. Intelligence is one such special field.

"Intelligence? Yes! But let's differentiate between police intelligence and the kind you hear about on the evening news. Police intelligence involves the kind of information-gathering that is related to the commission of a crime, or the prevention of one, such as murder, arson, or burglary. Police intelligence is necessary to plan a safe environment for the population, to enable to leaders of a community to prevent large-scale crimes such as dealing in drugs or narcotics.

"But there are other forms of intelligence. On the federal level, of course, we are not so much concerned with the commission or prevention of crime as with the kind of information needed to protect our Constitution and to prevent the erosion and subversion of our basic rights. Those are the true guardians of our freedom!

"Though basically a law enforcement agency, the FBI is most widely known in that category. The Mann Act, the Deyer Act, the Interstate Commerce Act. 'Hold it right there!' you scream. That's OK, you'll learn all about them if you join that special group. You have to have graduated from law school or be an accountant, if that's where your interests lie.

"Central Intelligence Agency. 'What do I need? How do I get in? Whom do I see? How do I prepare?' Well, as for the first question, nothing really. Nothing? Well, some good basic education plus a specialty currently in demand. Something like electronics, a language or two, and a major in psychology. Ethnic or cultural background and specialty education are the things that will open the doors for you there. More than that, they will take the doors off the hinges for you. Your college recruiter is the person to see if that's the kind of life that interests you most. As an intelligence officer your primary goal is to identify, predict, and possibly modify criminal or subversive behavior.

"Not all intelligence work is exciting. In fact, very little of it is in terms of public recognition. You are totally submerged in some profession, some activity not associated with what you are actually doing. However, personal satisfaction comes with accumulating life experiences and relationships with people of different origins, but most of all, in the knowledge that you are doing a job that few are able to do. For the broader-minded young student I would wholeheartedly recommend a career in government intelligence.

"So, you see, the difference between the various intelligence agencies is not really that great. They all have different objectives, and their activities are geared to accomplish that objective. Consequently, your role as an agent, or your life-style as an agent, is influenced by the broader goal of the agency that employs you. That is to say, if you want to stay in one place, want close contact with people on a daily basis, your local police department is the right choice. If, on other hand, you want travel and activity on a national level, still fighting crime, then the FBI is your future. But if you are the quiet type, one who observes rather than being observed; one who remains in the background but enjoys a mentally and emotionally stimulating life while performing some technical or specialty occupation; one who needs the fulfilling assurance of making a real contribution to the stability of our world, I can only suggest that some form of intelligence work may be the right environment for you."

# Further Reading

Cline, Ray S. *The CIA under Reagan, Bush and Casey.* Washington: Acropolis Books, 1981.

Felkenes, George T. *U.S. Law Enforcement.* Englewood Cliffs, NJ: Prentice-Hall, 1973.

Fox, William. *The Cop and the Kid.* New York: St. Martin's Press, 1983.

McAlary, Mike. *Buddy Boys; When Good Cops Turn Bad.* New York: Putnam, 1987.

McCarthy, Dennis V.N., with Phillip W. Smith. *Protecting the President.* New York: William Morrow, 1985.

Murray, Joseph A. *Police Officer.* New York: Arco, 1982.

Rush, George. *Confessions of an Ex-Secret Service Agent: The Marty Venker Story.* New York: Donald Fine, 1988.

Schroeder, Donald. *How to Prepare for the Police Officer Examination.* New York: Barron's Educational Series, 1982.

Whitehead, Don. *The F.B.I. Story.* New York: Random House, 1951.

Woodward, Bob. *The Secret Wars of the CIA.* New York: Simon & Schuster, 1987.

*Articles*

Broussard, Ginger, as told to Jean Libman Block. "I'm a Miami Vice Cop." *Good Housekeeping,* October, 1986.

Donham, Parker Barss. "Inferno on Queen Street," *Reader's Digest* (Canadian), December, 1987.

Snowden, Lynn. "Blues in the Night." *Interview,* August, 1988.

Urbanska, Wanda. "I Like to Get the Bad Guys," *McCall's,* February, 1989.

# Index